ADDING VALUE TO YOUR PRACTICE

DEMYSTIFYING ARCHITECTURAL RESEARCH

Anne Dye and Flora Samuel

RIBA ⊞ **Publishing**

Demystifying Architectural Research

© RIBA Enterprises Ltd, 2015

Published by RIBA Publishing, part of RIBA Enterprises Ltd, The Old Post Office, St Nicholas Street, Newcastle upon Tyne, NE1 1RH

ISBN 978 1 85946 578 3

Stock code 83983

The right of RIBA Enterprises Ltd to be identified as the Author of this Work has been asserted in accordance with the Copyright, Designs and Patents Act 1988 sections 77 and 78.

British Library Cataloguing-in-Publication Data

A catalogue record for this book is available from the British Library.

Publisher: Steven Cross

Commissioning Editor: Sarah Busby

Production: Richard Blackburn

Designed and Typeset by Gavin Ambrose

Printed and bound by CPI Antony Rowe in Chippenham, Great Britain

Cover design: Karen Wilks
Cover image © istock.com/ctriaplus1

RIBA Publishing is part of RIBA Enterprises Ltd.

www.ribaenterprises.com

Supporter

SSoA

The School of Architecture in the University of Sheffield is known for the excellence of its research and teaching as well as its strong links to practice. It is leading the development of Architectural Research Practice (ARP) in the UK because of its long-term commitment to social and environmental values. The development of evaluative techniques is key to understanding where and how best to use resources to improve the quality of our built environment. Evaluative techniques are also vital for demonstrating the contribution of our profession to society and to our economy. There is much to gain from the development of architecture's knowledge base, but it requires a cultural shift towards collaboration, not only between practice, academia and clients, but also with other disciplines and organisations beyond architecture's traditional concerns. Central to this is the development of a shared language, the fundamental aim of this book.

www.sheffield.ac.uk/architecture

Twitter: @SSoA_news

Foreword

Reading this book is an exciting voyage of discovery for any architect. The discovery that not only is it possible for a practice to gain a more in-depth understanding about a topic of personal or practice interest, but that many of us are already undertaking elementary research in our practices, unaware that this is what we are doing.

Unaware that with the right approach, collaboration with academia or other more experienced practices, or simply by trial and error, we may access funding which could elevate the innovative and stimulating original elements of the work which we enjoy. This, in turn, could create a unique marketing advantage, a USP which can draw clients towards us, enabling us to attract better more profitable projects.

The evidence is here that published and shared research, whether that research is done by a one man band or a large and established firm, can garner intellectual status, client reassurance and peers respect for a practice. It furthers the knowledge of the whole profession and can be a stepping stone to a more fulfilling and intellectual work life.

This easy to access, masterly and long awaited book by two of the architecture profession's leading research gurus, Anne Dye and Flora Samuel, uses case studies from a wide range of practices which tell their research stories first hand. It splits into the different genres of research to show us all the methods, the joys and the gains to be had: from more profit though commercial specialism, to a more altruistic contribution through sharing cultural and social knowledge.

The research projects themselves are an inspirational and uplifting read but, more than this, a clear message is spelled out throughout: do more research, indulge your passion, find funding, share your methods and results and your work will repay you many fold.

Let's get researching!

Jane Duncan
RIBA President 2015

Introduction

This book aims to help architects in practice to use research as a means to get ahead in business, to access new funding streams – almost €800 billion is currently available via the European Horizon 2020 programme – and to advance the knowledge economy of our field. We believe research to be key to helping architects regain some of the professional standing that has been eroded over time as D. Kirk Hamilton and David H. Watkins have observed:

It still stings: you are a respected architect, you've spent a great deal of effort attempting to convince your valued client about something, and you believed you were right ... Why does your client, who has worked with you before, not seem to trust your professional opinions?[1]

In writing this book we hoped to set out a compelling argument to show how engaging with research can help a client to win work, make a stronger case for fees and convince clients that the skills of an architect are of utmost importance to their project, while providing tools that will help them to design better buildings. Not only does research bring the business benefits of proven expertise and a unique selling point, it also brings great satisfaction as the architects who have contributed case studies to this book have shown.

Architecture is built on values that remain largely tacit. This puts the profession at a disadvantage when communicating with a public that have little understanding of what an architect does;[2] how can someone value the work that an architect does if they don't know what that work is? Countering this there is a growing body of practices that are using research to give clients evidence – as we all know, clients tend to like evidence – about why design makes a difference, and of how the practice is continually improving what they do. They are using research to define their brand, offer new services and improve how they work. At the same time they reap the rewards in terms of new or strengthened revenue streams. Many are small- to medium-sized practices with a strong presence in the regions, where business isn't bolstered by London's construction boom; practices like Architype, URBED and Bauman Lyons Architects have all contributed case studies. This book is for exactly this type of small- to medium-sized practice – the practices that make up the majority of architectural offices in the UK – so that they too can start to take advantage of the business benefits that research can bring.

The format of the case studies has been purposefully conceived to draw out the links between practice and more formally articulated forms of research.

The book:

- contains accounts – written by architects themselves – of how research is being used in practices across the country. We owe the contributors a great debt of gratitude; without them this book couldn't convey the glorious diversity of research in practice.
- draws on marketing knowledge, to help architects define and communicate the value of what they do, backed up with strong evidence.
- has sections to help architects get involved with research across a number of sectors (from understanding the context, to what methods you might use and who you might work with – plus of course how funding might be accessed).

When we started talking about writing the book it was from the standpoint of how we might best help architects to start to do research in their own practices. We had just worked together on a project – Home Improvements[3] – where we invited architects to join practice–academic–industry collaborative teams, tackling some of the thorny issues facing volume housebuilders today. We were excited by the enthusiasm of practices, but also concerned to find that many of the architects who expressed interest had little knowledge of the language of research which is rarely taught in any formal way in schools of architecture. How could we help practising architects to gain the skills and understanding needed to develop research, and to enjoy the satisfaction of proving the effectiveness of their practices in a language intelligible to non-architects including clients and policymakers? This book is the result of those conversations.

We detect a cultural shift within the profession towards innovation and knowledge exchange, as exemplified by Paul Morrell's recent report *Collaboration for Change*.[4] It is our hope that this book will contribute to this impetus by showing how practitioners up and down the UK and Ireland are already doing research even when they might not yet see it in those terms.

Anne Dye, RIBA Head of Technical Research
Flora Samuel, University of Reading

1   D. Hamilton & D.H. Watkins (2009) Chair of the RIBA Research and Innovation Group *Evidence Based Design for Multiple Building Types* (Wiley: New York)

2   YouGov (2012) 'An archi-what?' (YouGov: http://yougov.co.uk/news/2012/09/03/archi-what), (accessed 16 January 2014).

3   University of Sheffield School of Achitechture 'AHRC Home Improvements' (University of Sheffield: http://www.shef.ac.uk/architecture/research/homeresearch/home_research_projects/home_improvements, n.d), (accessed 28 July 2014).

4   Paul Morrell, *Collaboration for Change* (London: Edge). (www.edgedebate.com/wp-content/uploads/2015/05/150415_collaborationforchange_book.pdf) (accessed 20 June 2015).

About the editors

Anne Dye is Head of Technical Research at the RIBA, responsible for delivering the research agenda in alliance with the RIBA Research and Innovation Group. This includes the development, support and promotion of a range of strategic built-environment research projects within the RIBA, in partnership with other organisations and within the wider research community, as well as providing advocacy for research to key stakeholders.

Flora Samuel is an architect, Professor of Architecture and the Built Environment at the new School of Architecture in the University of Reading and former Head of the University of Sheffield School of Architecture. Her mission is supporting architectural practitioners in evidencing and communicating their value through research. She was recently awarded a research leader fellowship by the Arts and Humanities Research Council for 'Evidencing and Communicating the Value of Architects'. Her last project, Home Improvements – shortlisted for the 2014 RIBA President's Awards for Research – funded the production of the RIBA's report *Housing Research in Practice*, *The RIBA Research in Practice Guide* and the *RIBA SCHOSA Review of University Research*, as well as three practice collaborative projects with URBED, Ash Sakula and Satellite Architects. Samuel is Chair of the RIBA Research and Innovation Group and a founder member of the European research network ARENA, where her specialist area is Architecture Research Practice. She has published five books on Le Corbusier, two of them shortlisted for RIBA Research Awards. She also works as a consultant in developing research in practice.

Acknowledgements

The editors would like to thank all of the case study contributors to the book who have given their time and expertise, and so generously agreed to share their experience of research in practice. We are really pleased that so many of the practitioners found writing their case studies a thought-provoking process and an incitement to further developing the research aspects of their practices. We would also like to thank Fionn Stevenson, Julia Udall and Steven Walker – from Sheffield – for writing methods chapters for the book; we know their insights will help many architects as they start research projects in their own practices. Many thanks also to Penoyre and Prasad who allowed us to include images of their office at work. Sarah Busby at RIBA Publishing has provided invaluable editorial advice, and we are grateful for her help and for her unflagging enthusiasm.

Thanks must also go the RIBA Research and Innovation Group for supporting the book as part of their ongoing work to enable practicing architects to engage with and use research. This book and the projects that proceeded it would not have been possible without the benefit of Arts and Humanities Research Council Funding. We also thank the University of Sheffield for sponsoring the production of the book – without them the book would not exist.

The RIBA Research and Innovation Group works to champion built-environment research, innovation and knowledge. In particular it seeks to support architects in practice to develop their research skills and to develop the evidence base they need to win work, innovate, and meet current and future challenges. As well as working to disseminate research knowledge, the Group appoints the judging panel for the RIBA President's Awards for Research and the Research Medal, and convenes the annual RIBA Research Symposium as well as where practising architects, academics and other built-environment professionals come together to explore the issues that impact on the practice of architecture.

www.architecture.com/research

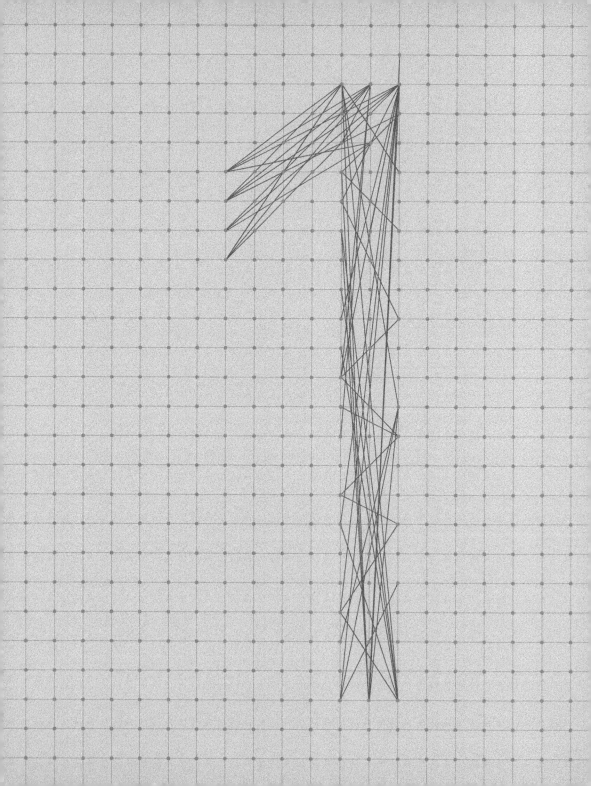

Part 1
Technological Research Practice

Chapter 1

DEMYSTIFYING TECHNOLOGICAL RESEARCH METHODS

FIONN STEVENSON, UNIVERSITY OF SHEFFIELD

CONTRIBUTOR PROFILE: FIONN STEVENSON

Fionn Stevenson holds a Chair in Sustainable Design and is Head of the University of Sheffield School of Architecture. Her research and consultancy work focuses on creating innovative methods of building performance evaluation in relation to occupancy feedback and social learning in order to improve building design.

CONTEXT

Good architecture is implicitly related to technological developments. While some aspects of technology have barely changed over the centuries (a brick is still a brick, for example) the exponential change in digital technologies has had a profound influence on construction, structural and environmental aspects of the building life cycle.

This chapter looks at some of the changes in the way technological and performance issues are approached, and relates them to research in practice. Finally it looks at where the industry may go in the future in response to the challenges posed by climate change.

CHANGING APPROACHES TO TECHNOLOGICAL AND PERFORMANCE ISSUES

Moving from building simulation to building performance

There is a long history of architects using empirical methods to test their design proposals, including physical models and prototyping, to help them understand potential performance outcomes. They rely on sound technical guidance when making design decisions, and use carefully constructed simulations to model how their buildings will perform (under particular conditions and use scenarios).

Yet post-occupancy evaluation (POE) shows that many buildings underperform on energy use, often by a factor of four, as the evaluative tools used may not be sufficient to resolve the complexity of the whole building. This difference between predicted and in-use energy consumption, often called the performance gap,[1] is becoming a key issue for clients and the design team, although POE has yet to become mandatory through Building Regulations. Clearly a critical approach to technology is essential to ensure that architecture performs well.

Sarah Wigglesworth Architects' exemplary primary school, Sandal Magna, demonstrates a unique attempt to 'demystify' the way the building works; visible environmental technologies are designed into the building to help occupants and visitors to read and use the building as a whole. The relationship between building and users has led to it being cherished, while also acting as a learning tool. Despite this, the complex technology employed at the school, and its command centre – the building management system (BMS) – have failed to perform as intended, due to a lack of adequate guidance and aftercare compounded by contractual difficulties. Such issues must inform a critical approach to the usability of technology, especially when recommending relatively complex technologies to clients and users. The move to a more holistic understanding of building performance represents a departure from more simplistic simulation of single issues.

Monitoring to socio-technical evaluation

Architects have always recognised the relationship between buildings and people, but it is only recently that they have begun to appreciate – based on the collection of sound evidence – the scale of the impact of human behaviour on actual building performance. At the ground-breaking BedZed development in Hackbridge, London, monitoring over the first seven years post-completion showed a twenty-fold variation in energy use for exactly the same housing design.[2] These types of studies have led a number of practices, such as Anne Thorne Architects, to actively adopt building performance evaluation methods which take account of people's attitudes and behaviour, in addition to the usability of the building itself.

Fabric performance standards

Another relatively recent change has been the increasing emphasis on improving the performance of the fabric of buildings. In the last few years an increasing number of practices have adopted the Passivhaus approach. Originating in Germany, the Passivhaus standards combine increased airtightness with high insulation standards in the building envelope, and controlled mechanical ventilation heat recovery systems.[3] The jury is still out on how resilient these technologies will be over time, but early performance evaluations have been very positive.

Other practices, such as Stride Treglown, are actively investigating the use of naturally hygroscopic materials (such as lime and hemp) to increase comfort, minimising the need to resort to mechanical air conditioning. New research and understanding of the building physics of natural materials is leading to an increasing interest in low embodied energy solutions for construction.[4]

Climate change mitigation and adaptation

Climate change prediction and modelling software[5] is becoming increasingly available and has the potential to be a game changer, offering practices – such as Bauman Lyons Architects (BLA) – the opportunity to future-proof their designs by factoring in predicted increases in temperature and extreme weather events, such as storms and flooding. By dealing with climate probabilities (rather than specific design constraints) this approach accepts a degree of uncertainty and leads to robust design solutions that can accommodate a range of different futures. It can be used to ensure that both new-build and retrofit projects are to remain fit for purpose.

BLA have made a commitment to do environmental modelling during the early stages of design, and aim to ensure that their design work is underpinned by a firm understanding of the building physics involved. This is something that all practices will need to do if they are to fully engage with the implications of our rapidly changing climate.

Economic life-cycle costing to whole life-cycle costing

The proportion of a building's total (embodied and in-use) energy consumption that happens before the building is even occupied can be between 30 and 70 per cent – and this has led to an increasing interest in moving from purely economic life-cycle costing to whole life-cycle costing, which includes embodied energy/carbon as well as other environmental impacts. These are methods that Stephen George & Partners have been investigating in their study of materials for 'commercial' projects. Despite increasing interest, there are no mandatory requirements to undertake this type of evaluation in the UK, although there is strong lobbying for change with proponents noting that whole life-cycle costing is routine in countries such as the Netherlands.[6]

Soft Landings and BIM

The last major change in technology is the advent of building information modelling (BIM) and the complementary Soft Landings process. Whereas BIM allows those involved to fully coordinate all aspects of building information over the building's whole life cycle, Soft Landings aims to help solve the performance gap.[7] The government is committed to applying Soft Landings through Government Soft Landings, mandated from 2016.[8]

TECHNOLOGICAL RESEARCH IN PRACTICE

Standards, simulation and the need to synthesise

Using technology successfully in architecture involves strategic briefing and the careful choice of performance targets, usually with the intention of meeting particular standards. While the choice of target standards is ultimately related to the client's ambitions, architects may influence the decision. Many practices prefer the BREEAM assessment as their benchmarking standard of choice, while others are increasingly adopting (and being employed because of their experience in meeting) standards that are more rigorous, or that focus on a particular aspect of performance. Like many practices, Anne Thorne Architects work to Passivhaus standards and use the related Passive House Planning Package (PHPP) spreadsheet tools during design.

While some standards have their own related tools, often the next step after standards are decided on is to choose a suitable building simulation software package, such as CarbonMixer,[9] which will allow preliminary morphological choices to be tested against predicted carbon emissions. Frequently a different package will be needed later in the design process in order to test and refine design proposals and predict overall energy and carbon use.

Selecting a detailed simulation is not always easy – there are many to choose from, and not all software is particularly user-friendly or well integrated with other design tools. However, judicious use of environmental software with climate change prediction tools, such as Integrated Environmental Solutions (IES) – as used by BLA for developing their future-proofed retrofit solutions, can pay huge dividends in terms of providing evidence to inform current design making. Nonetheless, through research associated with their modelling, BLA have identified numerous shortcomings with thermal simulation in relation to thermal adaptation strategies, which they have had to overcome in order to produce resilient solutions.[10]

Bucholz McEvoy Architects have taken their analysis further, and have developed a process which allows them to better synthesise their technical research. They know that with many design solutions come increasingly specific performance criteria relating to individual building elements and therefore use a matrix which allows them to make comparative judgements across multiple modes of working, recording data and criteria, to help ensure that they use technology holistically.

Embodied performance

Stephen George & Partners have taken a novel approach to assessing the various embodied factors contributing to fabric performance. Having identified the typical environmental criteria related to the whole life-cycle costing of materials, they go on to examine two factors they deem most important (embodied energy and carbon emissions) against other commercial factors such as delivery time, training requirements, potential product failure and financial risk. This allowed them to pragmatically rule out a number of materials for their case study building that had originally seemed environmentally promising. They also came to the conclusion that it was extremely difficult to obtain answers from manufacturers, suppliers and trade organisations and that it was unlikely that a single quantified answer could ever be arrived at. This is an interesting viewpoint, and one very much at odds with conventional evaluation tools, such as SimaPro or the BRE Green Guide to Specification.[11] It is also, perhaps, more honest, as it acknowledges the impact of context and location – something rarely present in typical life-cycle evaluation. However, the downside is that it is impossible to know how rigorous their evaluation actually is due to the 'swings and roundabouts' approach that effectively results in qualitative trade-offs. A truly comprehensive tool for materials selection, one that integrates both quantitative and qualitative issues, remains a holy grail.

Embodied energy is not the only aspect of building materials that requires research. Other aspects of the performance of materials include thermal properties; Stride Treglown are meticulous in their measurement of the thermal conductivity of materials, using desktop methods to predict the U-values of construction elements while monitoring performance through temperature and humidity data loggers. This allows them to analyse the performance of the insulation panels they have developed.

While none of the case studies in this section of the book has mentioned the use of thermal imaging cameras or airtightness testing, these are another two useful methods available to practices. Although not totally foolproof, they do give fairly quick answers about performance, flaws, and whether design intentions are being realised.

Building performance evaluation

Several of the case studies in this section have successfully utilised building performance evaluation (BPE) methods[12] to understand the performance of their projects in reality, and improve their future. BPE is different from POE in that its methods can be used at any stage of the building life cycle – not just after occupation – to inform future design and performance.[13] Unfortunately POE does not automatically result in performance improvement and, sadly, unless built in from the start, many studies are bolted on at the end, and their results may end up on the shelf. However BPE, or planned POE, can lead to useful findings.

Anne Thorne Architects used a variety of POE methods, including occupant surveys and environmental monitoring, to establish how well their design intentions were realised at Angela Carter Close. A key finding for them was about the importance of specifying environment controls for buildings that are more user-friendly. Stride Treglown Architects and Bucholz McEvoy Architects went one step further and investigated fabric design solutions by using BPE methods to improve performance directly.

Stride Treglown used careful experimental monitoring to test a new form of retrofit panelling. Bucholz McEvoy integrated BPE methods alongside prototyping and physical models to develop a bespoke timber facade for natural ventilation purposes. However, neither practice mentions evaluating the installation and commissioning stages: this can be critical when relating design intentions to actual performance.

FUTURE DIRECTIONS

If we are to survive the climate changes ahead and thrive in terms of human well-being, architects will need to rapidly embrace the idea not of zero carbon buildings, but of carbon positive environments. To avoid a catastrophic global temperature increase of four or even six degrees Celsius in the coming decades we need to use every means at our disposal. This includes designing buildings and environments that lock up (timber) and capture (titanium dioxide, foliage) carbon. Inevitably this will lead to a new, softer aesthetic for architecture as it moves from mechanical systems towards more socio-ecological systems as the principal drivers of design.

Energy production will become more resilient and localised; new buildings will need to produce more energy than they consume, to make up for the deficit of older, poorly performing buildings, so building integrated renewable energy will become important. Local material sourcing and production of buildings will become commonplace, through three-dimensional scanning and digital fabrication, helping to cut down on carbon-emitting transportation.

As we increasingly understand biomimicry and need to use less fossil fuel and smaller quantities of finite natural materials, building biology will become a mainstream preoccupation for architects. Our students will learn about BPE routinely in schools of architecture, and performance evaluation will be mandatory. We can expect cities to become urban forests of buildings that are more resilient than those produced today.

1   The Zero Carbon Hub has a large library which discusses this issue www.zerocarbonhub. org/full-lib

2   www.bioregional.com/bedzed-7-years-on/

3   www.passivhaustrust.org.uk

4   The Association for Sustainable Building Products has an excellent library of resources www.asbp.org.uk/resources/

5   The UK Climate Impact Programme (UKCIP) has a useful website wizard www.ukcip.org.uk

6   For example see Chapter 15 of W. Preiser & J. Vischer (2004), *Assessing Building Performance* (Abingdon: Routledge).

7   BSRIA (n.d.) *Soft Landings* (BSRIA: www.bsria.co.uk/services/design/soft-landings)

8   Cabinet Office (2013), *Government Soft Landings* (Cabinet Office: www.bimtaskgroup.org/ reports).

9   www.bobbygilbert.co.uk/CarbonMixer.html

10 For a good introduction to designing for climate change see: B. Gething & K. Puckett (2013), *Design for Climate Change* (London: RIBA Publications).

11 See the online tool available at www.bre.co.uk/greenguide

12 For a wide portfolio of performance evaluation methods see www.usablebuildings.co.uk

13 For an excellent introduction to what BPE is and how to do it see S. Mallory-Hill, W. Preiser & C. Watson (2012), *Enhancing Building Performance* (New York: Routledge Wiley-Blackwell).

Chapter 2

USER ENGAGEMENT AND TECHNOLOGICAL SELECTION IN AN INNOVATIVE GREEN SCHOOL BUILDING

SARAH WIGGLESWORTH, SARAH WIGGLESWORTH ARCHITECTS

CONTRIBUTOR PROFILE: SARAH WIGGLESWORTH

Sarah Wigglesworth is both a Professor of Architectural Practice at the University of Sheffield and an architect with her own practice in London. Her interests concern the integration of practice and theory. She established the MA in Design and Theory at Kingston University in 1994, and the PhD by Design at the University of Sheffield in 2002.

This project, for the design of a new primary school, aimed to pioneer design research that included engagement with the community as a central feature of its briefing and design process. Its goal was to extend our designs for our Building Schools for the Future (BSF) exemplar primary school by testing this brief in the context of the specific circumstances of this school community in Wakefield, Yorkshire. It further aimed to find out which low-energy strategies are viable for a school with little technical knowledge, and to test the effectiveness of our proposal for making the building a tool for teaching about sustainability.

Practice profile: Sarah Wigglesworth Architects
Sarah Wigglesworth Architects is a London-based architecture practice, founded 20 years ago. The practice works on education, residential, culture and community, public realm and mixed use, as well as on research.

The practice pioneered research through design and practice, starting with Stock Orchard St in 1996. The practice's research interests range from exploring a range of ecological design solutions, and the use of green technologies, to design strategies and critiques of prevailing architectural knowledge and discourse. They are interested in the interplay between creativity and systematic research process.

CONTEXT

In 2002 we designed a BSF exemplar primary school for the UK government, and were later commissioned by Wakefield Council to adapt its principles of sustainability, flexibility and a focus on individual-centred learning to address the needs of Sandal Magna Primary School. The design reflects the specific requirements of the community – high on the deprivation indices and with many children having special educational needs (SEN). With ambitions to become an Eco-School, the design sought to support the use of the building as a learning tool and aimed to be one of the lowest-carbon schools in the UK.

Our approach aimed to place user experience at the heart of the design process and address how the building could be low impact and low energy, establishing clearly which proposals worked and which did not.

APPROACH

We used stakeholder engagement and a rigorous testing and feedback method to evaluate and develop the designs, carrying out wide consultation with stakeholders over a period of about a year. These involved pupils, the Head and

Sandal Magna Primary School, 2011

the Deputy (who was also the Sustainability Champion), governors, teachers and the community, as well as the local authority. This knowledge formed the basis for developing an extended brief that encompassed research questions such as:

- How can the design address the needs of the specific cohort of pupils attending the school?
- How can the design incorporate passive environmental principles using the fabric of the building to control comfort conditions?
- How can the design support the school's status as an Eco-School, including assisting its sustainability curriculum?
- What procedures can we put in place for assessing and reviewing the building's performance?

Midway through the design development we received a grant from the Department for Education that meant the design could be augmented with new low-carbon technologies, leading to the following question:

- How can the design incorporate renewable technologies and how can we determine their contribution to energy saving?

INSIGHTS AND IMPACT

According to the head teacher the building exceeds the school's 'wants and needs', while providing a beautiful setting for learning and teaching that enables staff to develop their sustainability curriculum using the new building itself as a resource. The nursery was judged 'outstanding' in the 2012 Ofsted report, which specifically cited a measurable improvement in social, emotional and language development as being the direct result of the new building and its landscapes.

Sandal Magna has also won architectural recognition, winning an RIBA National Award as well as the RIBA Northern Network's Gold Award, Sustainability Award and Best Public Building in the Yorkshire Region Award.

The building's environmental effectiveness is the subject of a PhD at the University of Nottingham, and it has been reviewed extensively in a range of publications. Based on its passive design and low-carbon technologies Sandal Magna Primary School was predicted to have one of the lowest carbon footprints of any school in the UK. In practice, however, procurement processes, contractual disputes, equipment failure and the absence of an aftercare plan meant that there were some disappointments in the technical and managerial aspects of the building.

LESSONS

The design balances the specific needs of the school community – pupils, teachers, parents, local authority, community and those with SEN – with a cutting-edge design that is based on passive environmental principles, green technology, sophisticated environmental controls and innovative construction techniques. Socially the school has been very successful, welcoming mothers in particular into the community, between room and designing for parenting classes, and creating an atmosphere of support and nurturing, while enabling the eco-curriculum and day-to-day management of the green building and its systems. The school has now won three Eco-School flags.

The complex environmental controls and building management system (BMS) provided by additional grant money have proved more challenging for the school. In addition, difficulties with procurement systems, contractual disputes, faulty workmanship, IT problems and induction, training and aftercare in building management have meant that some aspects of the environmental strategy have not lived up to expectations. In future designs we will recommend passive design as well as familiar, simple, user-friendly methods for managing the comfort of the interior, and we will avoid costly and complicated technologies.

Chapter 3

MONITORING HOUSING IN USE

ANNE THORNE, ANNE THORNE ARCHITECTS LLP

CONTRIBUTOR PROFILE: ANNE THORNE
Anne Thorne is a founding partner at Anne Thorne Architects LLP. Her
approach to architecture is participatory. She was a founder and director
of Matrix Feminist Design Collective from 1981–8, pioneering an
approach focusing on women's unrecognised experience in the use and
understanding of the built environment.

The majority of the environment we live in has been designed by men, women have only fitted into it. As a women-led practice we have consistently aimed to consult and research on this and other social issues through all of our projects.

Anne Thorne Architects LLP is a small, women-led architectural practice of three partners working – through a participatory approach – on sustainable buildings and regeneration projects. Projects include schools, community buildings, sustainable housing refurbishment and new-build social housing. They are also currently involved in self-build and custom-build projects to Passivhaus standards.

The practice believes that buildings embody a statement of current trends – reflecting a changing society and a changing environment – and that through research it's possible to establish not only how buildings work and their capacity to control their internal environment, but also how the people who live in them use them. They view performance and behaviour as inseparable issues: for example, they found that installing solar-thermal water heating with electric back-up can be wasteful of electricity if users don't understand that the back-up should be switched off when not needed.

CONTEXT

Angela Carter Close – 12 attractive, eco-friendly houses and flats, completed in 2007 – was our first project with the Metropolitan housing partnership, who had an ambition to build greener homes. The aim was to build homes that would

The 'knuckle' of the terrace, built in breathing wall construction with English chestnut cladding

last, would be adaptable, and that would be as sustainable as possible; Lifetime Homes standard and a minimum EcoHomes rating of 'excellent' were sought. The scheme used timber frame construction, with 95 per cent of the wood being Forest Stewardship Council (FSC) certified, i.e. coming from a forest that is managed in line with the FSC's ten principles, which cover environmental, social and economic criteria.

As Metropolitan note, Angela Carter Close 'is only the second UK housing scheme to be certified by the Forest Stewardship Council. It has an impressive number of ecological features, including solar-thermal panels, to help cut energy bills. This once-derelict area of land, in one of London's most deprived wards, is now a beacon of sustainable best practice.'

But did the ratings match performance in use? We have worked with Dr Ben Croxford, senior lecturer on the Environmental Design and Engineering MSc at University College London (UCL), and his students to monitor several of our projects – to get hard data to explore the effect of our buildings on their inhabitants – and this was also done at Angela Carter Close.

APPROACH

Philosophy
We are concerned about our impact on the planet, from the embodied carbon in building materials, to the effect on individuals' health and well-being, particularly those in fuel poverty. Because of this we wanted to get data on some of our schemes – including Angela Carter Close – to establish how our buildings work. The essential question for the research to answer was 'How do the buildings perform in use?'

Methods
Two methods were chosen for the research; physical monitoring and occupant surveys.

Physical data collected included primary energy consumption – gas and electricity – for five housing schemes. The resulting dataset was compared to average UK consumption data (from the Technology Strategy Board, 2009), unless pre- and post-refurbishment data for our buildings was available. The results are notional energy and CO_2 emissions savings.

Comparative data was used rather than predicted figures from SAP calculations, as these are not able to predict the impact of user occupancy patterns, and so can give much lower estimates for energy use. Instead comparisons were made across usage between similarly sized homes/households.

INSIGHTS AND IMPACT

Polyxeni Tzachrista worked with us on the research on Angela Carter Close for her MSc dissertation – 'Why is the actual operating energy use of low energy UK homes higher than designed?' – in 2009. She found that 'increased thermal comfort requirements, lifestyle and above all a lack of communication between physical systems and humans were identified as the motives underlying the inefficient use of space heating systems'. Her research highlighted the importance of providing homes with simple, clear design solutions as well as providing occupants with effective advice and guidance on how to exploit the potentials of a low energy design. Factors found to affect a household's energy use included:

- **Internal temperature:** A 2°C reduction in thermostat set point can lead to up to a 20 per cent reduction in energy use.
- **Ventilation use:** Good practice can save up to 30 per cent of space heating energy.
- **Occupant behaviour:** Hours of occupation can be very different, for e.g. if a tenant is disabled and spends the majority of their time at home.

LESSONS

A number of lessons for future design came from our research at Angela Carter Close:

- Design to ensure control interface simplicity (so occupants can use systems easily).
- Fine turning of energy systems is required prior to handover.
- Commissioning problems can occur – plan for them.
- At handover provide advice and guidance on how to exploit the potential for low energy use – provide motivation to residents by clear and simple solutions.
- Ensure any malfunctions after handover are identified.
- After handover assess operation by residents – and provide additional guidance if necessary.
- Provide energy consumption displays – ignorance of energy consumption can lead to indifference.

Through our work on this scheme, and other projects, we realised that the Passivhaus standard delivers more user-friendly outcomes than conventionally designed homes and results in homes that do not require much maintenance and cost as little as the cost of a cup of coffee per fortnight to heat. The fabric-first approach reduces the need for complicated heating systems – and where they are necessary, straightforward, user-friendly controls are important.

Chapter 4

ADAPT AND SAVE – CLIMATE ADAPTATION STRATEGIES

IRENA BAUMAN, BAUMAN LYONS ARCHITECTS

CONTRIBUTOR PROFILE: IRENA BAUMAN
Irena Bauman is a Founding Director of Bauman Lyons Architects and has been Professor of Sustainable Urbanism at the University of Sheffield School of Architecture since 2012. Her diverse research interests relate to the role and work of the architect, as well as the impact of architecture and the built environment, with particular reference to sustainability and the environmental, social and economic futures of buildings and communities.

---

initially our practice-based research was commissioned by a Regional Development Agency, but subsequently we began to raise our own research funding. Our interest in the impact of climate change on buildings and on urban design was inspired by work on the futures of market towns. In the last four years we have secured two separate research grants from Innovate UK (previously the Technology Strategy Board) – under the Climate Adaptation Strategies call – to develop an understanding of how commercial buildings could be adapted to respond to overheating caused by climate change, and whether such adaptation was commercially viable. The total grant was £200,000, with £120,000 allocated directly to the practice. The Adapt and Save project was part of this work on adaptation strategies.

Practice profile: Bauman Lyons Architects

Bauman Lyons is a small architectural practice with eight staff, established in 1992. Based in Leeds, the practice has a policy of only working on projects within two hours' travelling distance of the office.

The practice works on both domestic and commercial projects, preferring projects that they believe add value to the community. They also undertake feasibility studies, master planning and community planning.

New knowledge is constantly evolving and the practice looks to engage with it through research activities. They see their work as an investigation of new strands of knowledge which they then apply to practice through new tools, processes and building typologies. They actively investigate alternative methods of scholarship, which they see as enhancing the impact of their architectural work.

CONTEXT

It was a condition of the research funding that a live project of £3 million in construction value was available to be used as a case study. We had already been commissioned to convert a disused arts college in Doncaster into a 6,000m² creative work space, with an anticipated construction value for the refurbishment of £6.2 million. The research developed and tested adaptation strategies for the project.

The Adapt and Save project was to investigate the impact of global warming and climate change on the overheating of existing commercial buildings, and to develop an approach to the production of commercially viable adaptation strategies that could be widely replicable and would allow the subject buildings to provide comfortable environmental conditions up to the year 2080 without resorting to mechanical cooling and air conditioning.

We led a multidisciplinary team that comprised: Arup, Estell Warren Landscape Architecture, facility managers Creative Space Management, as well as the client group and a number of climate change experts.

> **Research and Bauman Lyons Architects**
> Change is the constant condition which requires architects to plug themselves into emerging knowledge. Bauman Lyons are not innovators, but early adopters. They investigate new strands of knowledge and apply it to their practice by devising new tools, processes and building typologies. Bauman Lyons actively pursue a number of alternative scholarship methods to enhance the reach of their architectural work.

APPROACH

Philosophy

The construction industry has made great advances in developing mitigation strategies to reduce CO_2 emissions, but the understanding of adaptation lags some ten years behind. As we come to terms with the inevitability of climate change we also need to start developing an understanding of how to adapt our physical environment for greater resilience to the changes that are already in motion. To develop this new knowledge requires co-created research across the professions with users and facility managers. It also requires challenging some of the current industry assumptions about office occupancy patterns, and policies – such as the current Building Regulations requirements – that commit us to greater problems in the future.

Methods

We used research by design as the method to identify a series of physical, management and behavioural adaptations and anti-adaptations which were then developed as a taxonomy. Each adaptation was modelled in Integrated Environmental Solutions (IES) software throughout the iterative design process; modified, modelled again, priced, morphed with other adaptations set against a time line and finally evaluated through whole life-cycle costing, and put through a sensitivity analysis. Throughout the research newly available data (such as the weather files and climate projections offered in UKCIP02)[1] was interpreted and sensitively tested.

INSIGHTS AND IMPACT

The innovations from the project included identification of 12 building adaptations (and three types of mal-adaptation), enabling the incremental integration of climate change adaptation into the building design and into future maintenance cycles so adaptations can be applied as they become necessary. The taxonomy of adaptations can be used for developing adaptation strategies for a wide range of buildings. Findings suggest that high ceilings, high thermal mass and cross-ventilation – with windows sized and designed to take account of orientation – can prevent overheating now and in the future. Many existing buildings with air-conditioning systems can be adapted to mitigate the need for mechanical cooling.

The taxonomy of adaptations was also a helpful tool in evaluating whether the building was suitable for adaptation in the first place; it could also be used on other buildings in the future. This provides an important framework for decision-making about investment in the refurbishment of buildings.

The knowledge from the project has changed the way Bauman Lyons practises: we do our own environmental modelling during the early stages of design and charge a fee for the service – met from the M&E design budget. The research has also led to further successful research applications. It has been published, used as a best-practice exemplar, and was nominated for an RIBA President's Award for Research in 2013.

LESSONS

The impact of this study is far-reaching, as it provides new knowledge and understanding of an unexplored field. Furthermore, the research calls into question some current regulatory trends such as the increasing of airtightness and levels of insulation in buildings, as well as the planning systems which currently restrict – especially in Conservation Areas – the modifications that need to be made to buildings to adapt them for climate change. The research also exposed the inadequacy of the tools available for modelling thermal comfort, as they cannot model some key adaptations, such as shading by plants, the albedo effect[2] and the cooling effect of ceiling fans, and they do not account for basic considerations such as the inability to ventilate through roof lights during rain.

The impact on Bauman Lyons was significant; we now aim for designs to be underpinned by a real understanding of building physics and the changing environmental context. We are planning further research, teaching and dissemination of the knowledge we have gained and we feel we have something significant and positive to contribute to the field.

Church View, Doncaster, West Elevation, 1930s Arts College, Climate Change Adaptation to the building would allow it to be weaned off the current reliance on air-conditioning

1   M. Hulme et al (2002), *Climate Change Scenarios for the United Kingdom: The UKCIP02 Scientific Report* (Norwich: Tyndall Centre for Climate Change Research, School of Environmental Sciences, University of East Anglia). UKCIP02 has now been superseded by the UKCP09 probabilistic projections. See UK Climate Projections, Glossary: ukclimateprojections.metoffice.gov.uk.

2   The impact of the amount of incoming solar radiation that is reflected back to space.

Chapter 5

INFORMATION SYSTEMS FOR TECHNICAL DESIGN

MERRITT BUCHOLZ, BUCHOLZ MCEVOY ARCHITECTS

CONTRIBUTOR PROFILE: MERRITT BUCHOLZ
Merritt Bucholz is a Founding Director of Bucholz McEvoy Architects. His interests in practice include research and development in design, building technology and energy systems. He has also been a visiting professor at Harvard University, and has lectured at Princeton, Cornell, the School of Architecture at University College Dublin and Dublin Institute of Technology.

B uildings often take years to settle into a pattern of use in terms of energy and occupant behaviour. By examining a building after a long span of time, in this case ten years, the building's performance can be evaluated against the very tightly defined environmental performance that governed the original design process. Using a comprehensive analytical method, the building's performance and use can be optimised to exceed the expected reduction in energy costs.

Practice profile: Bucholz McEvoy Architects
Bucholz McEvoy Architects is a small architectural practice based in Dublin, Ireland. They work with both public and private clients on projects at a variety of scales, from furniture to urban quarters.

The practice's research is conducted in collaboration with the School of Architecture at the University of Limerick and PAC Studio Architects. The university partner helps to establish clear research methodologies and provides a structured, unbiased and critical framework, while partnering with another architectural practice provides a broader set of analytical skills.

CONTEXT

Developing an effective, elemental and whole-building performance design research method is essential when the building fabric replaces mechanical environmental systems, and passive design principles govern all design decisions. A focused research methodology was needed in order to effectively design within a narrow set of performance parameters for each part of the building fabric. In order to address this issue we have, since 2008, been developing a method to identify and track performance holistically, from the beginning of the design process through to the long-term use of a building.

APPROACH

Philosophy
Our research is grounded in performance. Every refinement of the design solution contains increasingly specific performance criteria relating to individual building elements composed of bespoke details. We refer to this design research as 'synthesising technical research'. It enables the construction of polyfunctional architectural assemblies whose performance is analysed under functional, technological, environmental and aesthetic criteria.

Methods
At Limerick County Hall a bespoke timber facade with timber structure, timber mullions and cladding panels employing multiple species of timber was used to

naturally ventilate a diverse set of interior functions, including municipal buildings and offices. Our research effort was directed towards breaking down and synthesising the separate functional requirements of the components of the building fabric that act together as the primary environmental machine for the building: structural elements, environmental systems, and spatial and weathering elements. These were treated as a holistic and complex ensemble of performing elements. Then they were tested for performance in terms both of energy use and occupant enjoyment ten years after the project was completed.

The design process went through a set of steps, now familiar to the practice, starting with setting boundary conditions and establishing performance criteria. Design research through drawing, simulations, and models that cross between environmental, structural and architectural issues followed. Finally prototypes were built and went through a series of tests, for example at the Centre for Window and Cladding Technology.

The post-occupancy evaluation commenced eight years after the building was completed and went on for two years. This ensured that no residual issues relating to the construction process informed the research, and that the organisation was familiar with the building. Evaluation methods included:

- **Monitoring:** Temperature data loggers were located throughout the building, recording temperatures in four key work spaces on each floor and in the public atrium spaces. There was also an external temperature sensor as a reference. The output from these data loggers is presented month by month, and floor by floor, as temperature graphs tracing the diurnal changes in temperature for each floor relative to the ambient external temperatures. Specific differences between the spaces or between the floors highlight issues with building fabric/occupation/ ventilation relative to the demands on the heating systems.
- Monthly visits to the building provided the opportunity for further specific **data harvesting techniques** – humidity, temperature and carbon dioxide monitors were used to record the specific environments on each floor, on a 'datagrid' of six metres. This data was translated into graphical format, showing the changes in environmental conditions on each floor plate, at a moment in time. Factors affecting the environmental conditions were mapped on these plans, including the weather conditions, position of the sun, and the deployment of blinds and opening windows, radiators and extractor fans, along with the occupancy levels.
- Two methods of **surveying the behaviour and views** of the building occupants were deployed. Monthly visits by the research team provided the opportunity to informally discuss any issues with the staff, from a particular draught issue in a work space, to the need for more control over heating and cooling. An extensive questionnaire was devised in conjunction with the client and issued via a discrete web interface. This surveyed the level of perceived control and variation in environmental comfort for

employees. Wider issues (traffic, catering, etc.) were also raised. The staff were free to voice other concerns and make suggestions within the survey.

- **Simulation:** a building energy model was established using a thermodynamic analytical software package that employs parametric routines to simulate the performance of the building fabric relative to historic Shannon weather files, actual building occupancy loads, building fabric, orientation and geometry. The calibration of lighting systems, user loads and heating demand/fabric losses has enabled various improvement strategies to be tested.

INSIGHTS AND IMPACT

The overall impact of this research has been the improved energy performance of the building to the point where it exceeds the targets set at design stage for energy usage, by a substantial margin. In Limerick County Hall the energy bill was reduced by 50 per cent over this two-year process. This was distributed equally between savings in electricity and natural gas for heating.

A renewed interest and education in the principles of passive-usage of the passively designed building increased the satisfaction and productivity of the building's occupants. Though most of them had worked in the building for at least ten years most had forgotten its energy saving design.

As an approach that is distinct from designing to achieve benchmarks, design-synthesised building fabric achieves continuous energy reductions over the lifetime of a building's use. This suggests that a new and environmentally functional aesthetic should govern many design decisions.

LESSONS

The process of tuning the operation of the building fabric by automated building management systems needs to evolve towards control by smaller user groups, and improved responsiveness as more data about physical state becomes available.

Granularity and resolution of predictive modelling at the design stage needs to be re-calibrated against real-life performance. Increased granularity in design-stage simulations needs to be mirrored with increased level of control over day-to-day operation. This contributes to a culture of seasonal operation and adjustment, and continuous learning as climates change. High performance is the result of robust – and continuous – integration of occupant behaviour into the energy strategy of the building, over a long time frame.

Limerick County Hall

Chapter 6

SUSTAINABLE BUILDING MATERIALS FOR COMMERCIAL DEVELOPMENTS

CHRIS HALLIGAN AND STEPHEN GEORGE & PARTNERS LLP

CONTRIBUTOR PROFILE: CHRIS HALLIGAN

Chris Halligan is a former director with Stephen George & Partners and chaired the practice's steering group on sustainability, design and technology. In 2011, with colleague Joanne Denison, he won the RIBA President's Award for Outstanding Practice-located Research for producing *The Stephen George & Partners Guide to Building Materials and the Environment*.[1]

O ur 2009 Sustainable Construction training and research centre project (Sus-Con) was for a public–private partnership led by Dartford Borough Council, Prologis UK Ltd and North West Kent College. It was intended that the building itself should be a learning tool for sustainable construction. In addition to employing both passive strategies and renewable technologies, the clients wanted a range of sustainable and innovative materials to be used in its construction in a manner which would allow them to demonstrate how such materials might be used on other commercial projects.

Practice profile: Stephen George & Partners
Stephen George & Partners LLP was founded in 1970 and has around 60 staff in offices in London, Leicester, Leeds and Solihull, with subsidiary offices in Sofia, Bulgaria and Salalah, Oman. They work in both the private and public sectors, covering a wide range of building types.

The practice began engaging in research early in its history. In 1978 it was commissioned to research passive solar energy collection by the European Economic Community (now the European Union). They continue their interest in research and sustainable design today, believing that not only do architects have a degree of social responsibility, but that through investigation and expanding knowledge architects can ensure that their designs help to make the world a better place.

CONTEXT

As chair of our sustainability steering group I was asked by the partner in charge of the SusCon design team to assist in the resolution of the environmental strategy and to create a palette of sustainable materials for the project. In terms of likely materials we very quickly found our preconceptions challenged: it became obvious that many of the potential materials had rarely been employed in a commercial environment. Where they had been used it was often in a one-off domestic or demonstration project. Further, much of the expertise related to the materials seemed to reside at the 'enthusiast' level and not with commercial suppliers or contractors.

APPROACH

Philosophy
We wanted to promote the use of sustainable materials within so-called commercial projects through an investigation of materials commonly used for this type of project as well as those considered 'green'. This approach to sustainable materials differed from preceding work in the field.

Methods

We wanted to consider every aspect of the manufacturing and use of a building material which might be considered to relate to environmental impact, and found it necessary to set a datum in order to compare various materials with one another. For us sustainability encompasses the following issues:

- Low embodied energy
- Contribution to energy saving in use
- Low pollution (during manufacture and in use)
- Low toxicity
- Recycled content
- End-of-life options
- Low resource depletion
- Social issues

We eventually took the view that the issue of embodied energy and the contribution to climate change should form the focus of our assessments, but with adequate recognition of the other issues. Next a wide range of materials was explored, largely in terms of commercial issues such as the following:

- How long would delivery take?
- How much material could be delivered?
- Would specialised training be required for the main contractor's workforce?
- Would use of the material require a longer site programme?
- Would there be an increased risk of failure?
- Who would we have to ask to accept that risk, and what would be the financial and contractual impact?

To our surprise the answers to some of these questions resulted in us rejecting several of our preferred materials and led us to investigate and consider commonly available alternatives.

INSIGHTS AND IMPACT

Our initial findings were that it was extremely difficult to obtain the answers we were seeking – even from manufacturers, suppliers and trade organisations. Furthermore it was unlikely that a single quantified answer could ever be arrived at. Once all issues of sustainability were considered each material would only be considered against the others on the basis of 'swings and roundabouts', and then in a specific context. The project did however enable us to make more informed decisions on the SusCon project. It occurred to me that if we had experienced such trouble in specifying sustainable materials, other people might be having the same difficulties. I persuaded the practice partners to let me expand the research, and to

The SusCon Academy in Dartford, Kent, inspired the idea for the research project and provided the initial study vehicle for various materials.

collate the findings into the work that eventually became *The Stephen George & Partners Guide to Building Materials and the Environment*, which we made freely available as a web-based resource.

LESSONS

Beyond the intrinsic technical conclusions of the study, the research has provided the practice with a demonstrable understanding of the sustainability of building materials beyond that which might normally be expected. This should provide us with a clear commercial advantage – especially when we are lucky enough to work for more enlightened clients.

We didn't undertake the research for its own sake: it had a practical application. Although I hoped that the *Guide* would help to minimise the building industry's impact on our planet, I was also aware that it would demonstrate and advertise our knowledge and expertise in what was then a relatively new field, leading to further commissions for innovative and exciting projects.

1   C. Halligan & J. Denison (2010), *The Stephen George & Partners Guide to Building Materials and the Environment*. (Stephen George & Partners).

Chapter 7

PERMEABLE INSULATION AND POWER

IAN STANDEN, STRIDE TREGLOWN

CONTRIBUTOR PROFILE: IAN STANDEN

Ian Standen is an architect with over 25 years' experience in architectural practice and in higher education. At the Welsh School of architecture he was Associate Director of the Project Office, involving a leading role in the academic provision of practice within research and teaching by undertaking projects providing live test beds for research-derived ideas.

---

n January 2014, the City of Cardiff Council launched a competition funded by Innovate UK and the Welsh government's Small Business Research Initiative (SBRI) invited proposals for innovative energy-saving ideas compatible with traditionally constructed heritage buildings, generally pre-1919.

Permeable insulation and power (PIP) is a new technology that applies cutting-edge low-power coated electrical heating to permeable prefabricated lime-based internal wall insulation in existing buildings. The primary aim is to enhance the insulation and energy performance of the building, affecting its external appearance, thereby reducing building running costs. Research has shown that traditionally constructed walls allow moisture to flow through the wall which means that compatible permeable insulations materials are needed. The lime-based insulation used in this approach is known for its permeable qualities. This ancient material is combined with the latest development in low-powered conductive coatings, effectively turning the wall surface into a large radiator ensuring that the building occupants are comfortable. The PIP feasibility study was carried out in collaboration with other innovative companies including Vivus Lime Ltd, Okatech Ltd, the BioComposites Centre at Bangor University and Wood Knowledge Wales.

Practice profile: Stride Treglown

Founded in 1953, Stride Treglown is a practice of around 270 with nine offices in the UK and in the UAE. They work in architecture, interior design, BIM, master planning and urban design, landscape architecture, town planning, building surveying, historical building conservation, project management, BREEAM/environmental assessment, sustainable design, CDM/health and safety, and graphic design.

The practice engages with research in order to respond to changing building technologies, and the burgeoning number of products and systems available – buildings are becoming increasingly complex entities, with occupant health and well-being key to architectural success. Evaluation of product suitability requires in-depth understanding of, for example, material composition and microclimatic conditions within constructions and spaces, so Stride Treglown's business plan has allocated funds for research activities. Research knowledge is disseminated within the practice and made available to inform future projects.

Dr Bruce Philip setting up the monitoring equipment for the low conductive heated panels used in the PIP project

CONTEXT

An experimental room was used within an existing privately owned eighteenth-century stone-built cottage in Monmouthshire. The building showed typical conditions of cold, damp walls, resulting in uncomfortable internal conditions for occupants. The project drew inspiration from various existing research, including doctoral research work by Gary Perkins at Cardiff Metropolitan University into admixtures and mix proportions, Bruce Philip's work at Swansea University on autonomous buildings, and John Counsell's building performance evaluation with Cadw (the Welsh government's historic environment service) at Heritage Cottage, Cwmdare.

APPROACH

Philosophy

Our aim was to improve energy performance within a traditional building while leaving its essential character intact. We attempted to achieve this using everyday skills, low to intermediate technology and a skill base for construction industry small and medium enterprises (SMEs) with readily available auditable recording sensors and data logging.

Methods

The project programme was divided into the following stages:

- **Design stage:** Firstly the formulation of numerous mixes of hemp lime was explored – this had appeared, through previous research to offer the possibility of forming prefabricated hemp panels. A six-week iterative design stage followed, including sourcing suitable materials in conjunction with developing mould designs. A prototype panel 45mm thick resulted in thermal conductivity of 0.09874 watts per square metre per degree Celcius ($W \cdot m^{-1} \cdot K^{-1}$) when tested at Bangor University. A desktop calculation, assuming an existing solid stone wall of 400mm with lime plaster interior finish, indicated a U-value in the region of 1.55 watts per square metre per degree Celcius. By adding the hemp/lime units we predicted that the rate of heat loss from the space would improve by 50 per cent, with a U-value of 0.8237 watts per square metre per degree Celcius.
- **Installation:** The installation stage began with a laser scanned survey of the experimental room, the removal of existing finishes, making good the walls, installation of the hemp/lime panels and two conductive coated panels (one surface mounted room side, and the other embedded between the hemp panel and the existing stonework) and connection of room monitoring equipment fixed internally and externally.
- **Monitoring:** The test chamber was monitored with remote access from August 2014 until March 2015, and computer data was downloaded via a webpage link and a low-cost Raspberry Pi computer located within the room.

INSIGHTS AND IMPACT

The project has successfully combined a low-powered heating system with permeable lime/hemp insulation to provide a potential solution to the damp, cold conditions often experienced in older, solid construction buildings. Two design approaches compared a surface-mounted radiant-heated panel with one embedded in the wall providing thermal mass.

A full analysis of the data was undertaken at the end of March 2015, with results published both within each organisation and in external technical publications.

LESSONS

The key feature of the project is breathability. The hygroscopic hemp/lime insulation units provide a material lining capable of managing moisture in the building where some modern materials (such as gypsum plaster) cannot.

Introduction of material of this nature could lead to indoor air-quality improvements for the occupants, energy saving, and life-cycle benefits for the building owner as the materials are recyclable and environmentally benign. The use of responsive sensor-linked heated panels provides the user with better control over changing room conditions through the seasons.

Our advice to others considering undertaking research of this nature is:

- Do not underestimate the time required to develop innovative ideas.
- Keep to your budgets by firm project management.
- When working in collaboration or consortium, make sure roles and responsibilities are fully agreed and understood with appropriate IP rights in place.

The benefits to practice and individuals involved are immeasurable, as first-hand knowledge of making and doing dispels the myth that surrounds the use of traditional materials in construction such as lime.

Part 2
Social
Research
Practice

Chapter 8

DEMYSTIFYING SOCIAL RESEARCH METHODS

JULIA UDALL, UNIVERSITY OF SHEFFIELD

CONTRIBUTOR PROFILE: JULIA UDALL

Julia Udall is a postgraduate design tutor at Sheffield School of
Architecture, and a director of Studio Polpo. She is currently part of the
AHRC Connected Communities project 'Stories of Change', which aims to
help to revive stalled public and political conversations about energy
by looking in a fresh way at its past, present and future.

CONTEXT

Socially motivated architectural practices aim to transform the spaces and buildings people use and care about. Often they have a strong commitment to equality, sustainability and social justice, and research in this field supports these aims, valuing lived experiences and non-professional forms of expertise. Their research contributes to the questioning of assumptions, values and received ways of doing by working to create agency in communities and with clients.

This chapter explores activities that have elements of socially motivated research, through the work of architectural researchers who have combined visual, cartographic[1] and design methodologies with approaches drawn from management, education[2] and community development (such as Participatory Action Research,[3] advocacy[4] and cooperative enquiry[5]), to create a range of methods useful for the field. These approaches emerged in the 1960s in response to calls for a more politicised and socially engaged design practice, within the context of wider struggles. Marxist philosopher Henri Lefebvre's[6] work on the 'right to the city' and the 'social production of space' is incredibly influential for many when thinking about these concerns. Lefebvre argues for our right to continually and radically remake ourselves as a society through remaking our urban realm.

Before looking at socially motivated research in practice it is useful to consider how the practices who undertake it – and the way they fund their work – are changing.

Changing practices

Increasingly architectural practices are choosing to employ a more diverse range of staff, to include professionals such as economists, artists, creative practitioners and town planners, often in non-hierarchical or cooperative practice structures. This breadth of expertise brings additional methods to enable a better understanding of points of intervention and leverage (for example in policy, funding or development plans), and an opportunity to critically reflect on how architects are embedded in certain structures and ways of working.

By unlocking funding opportunities in the charity, arts, heritage or educational sectors, practices can initiate projects,[7] and choose to work with groups who may not usually have access to architectural services. In this way it is possible to generate new sources of income that are not market-reliant, enabling attention to be given to issues and concerns that may not be the subject of commercially focused projects.

ELEMENTS OF SOCIALLY MOTIVATED RESEARCH

These sections look at the elements that make up a socially motivated architectural research practice project. The project may or may not include a design element (co-design and proposing alternatives) and the other elements may have very different weighting from project to project, and may use quite different research methods (highlighted in bold in the sections below) within them – some of which are discussed here. A vital part of all research is its ethical framework, and consideration of this is the first element of any research project.

Considering the ethical framework
Research should be conducted with honesty, integrity and respect for those with whom you work, or who may be affected by your activities. Being open about what you are doing and why – and checking throughout the process that those involved are still comfortable with taking part – is central to this. Formalised risk assessments and ethics procedures[8] are a useful way to ensure that these principles are being adhered to, and these can be shared publicly to allow for scrutiny and feedback.

Understanding and representing project context
Central to socially motivated research is a careful and close understanding of the people and places with which you are working as well as their context-for-action. Critiques of consultation and participation in architecture, planning and urbanism suggest that it is crucial to work with and from communities, rather than relying on simplistic or preconceived notions of identity or what matters to people. Through working collectively to understand how a space is used, to map stakeholders, and to understand what the concerns and opportunities are, you can develop a brief that is embedded in a place.

It is important for a practice to *go to* the people they are working with, both in terms of selecting places in which they are comfortable and using language that is not littered with jargon. Attention should be paid to who is invited to take part in activities, and who feels confident to contribute in a particular context. In diverse communities it is likely that this will vary, so often using a number of different methods enables a broader range of people to engage more fully.[9] It should not be assumed that a community exists as a coherent entity because of proximity[10] or is necessarily defined by the boundary of a neighbourhood. Research methods such as storytelling, taking group walks or joining in with local events can allow for a more open and complex representation of a place.

Cottrell & Vermeulen explain that they work in neighbourhoods close to their practice in order to build long-term relationships and to build an understanding of local policies and urban strategies that influence their framework for producing a project. They aim to develop architecture that is particular to the communities, relationships and needs of a place. Through bringing together teaching and practice, they set out an approach that is driven by exploration and experimentation. Particularly through their work at schools, this involves groups coming together to speculate and imagine alternative futures, by collaging, modelling, making short films and talking together.[11]

In writing about her approach to house design, Jane Burnside speaks about how demographic changes such as the increase in single-person households and blended families should impact on brief development, challenging assumptions about lifestyle and relationships. Through asking clients to gather images that represent their desires and needs she seeks to explore the relationship of the design of their home to their sense of identity and the way they conduct their everyday lives. She emphasises listening over speaking and positions herself as a therapist rather than a theorist, building knowledge with the client that articulates how the programme should be expressed. These kind of processes take time and care, but if successful can lead to the development of strong relationships and the production of rich and engaging feasibility and development work.

Building networks and relationships

Closely allied to understanding the context of a project is the need to build networks and connections beyond the client or user group. Working with existing groups and organisations 'on the ground' allows a practice to gain specialist local knowledge and make relationships which would otherwise take significant time to build. There is sometimes an inclination to start from scratch, but often others have done valuable work already, and raking over old ground can lead to consultation fatigue and wasted energies. Through critically reviewing reports, surveys and information that is 'already out there' you can identify gaps or opportunities (using your time more efficiently) while bringing your own analysis of the issues raised to the table. In building on what others have done you can build respect, and work in more nuanced ways to produce ideas that are relevant to the situation in which you are working.

John Sampson of URBED stresses the ethical importance of participatory processes that continue over a long period, with a number of iterations of design work being repeatedly 'taken back' into the community for critique and further development. He considers design research a useful way to formulate a particular approach – responding to a need or opportunity – that can then be marketed as a service. In order to ensure the approach is the right one for the job, URBED works collaboratively with other practices and with specialist educational and campaigning organisations. This approach leads to the production of many different kinds of output, from publications, to talks and events, each appropriate to their audience and aims. Working in this way can strengthen the resilience of a project by networking and allying it with people with different skills, capacities and resources. Improving your connections in this way can help you practise developing future collaborations, and broaden your potential client base.

Developing skills and proficiencies

Socially motivated architectural research can support clients and communities to develop skills and proficiencies necessary to change things they are concerned about be it a neighbourhood, a park, a street or a building. This could include things as varied as understanding planning processes or legal rights, how to commission artists, understanding social history, the political context of local regeneration policies, or how to write a funding bid. Through meetings and conversation you develop an understanding of the skills that already exist in a community, which skills are needed to achieve shared goals and how people can come together to learn effectively from one another. The aim is to empower communities to be able to create change, and to build sustainability and future opportunities. Research methods that enable this include the development of workshops, hosting talks and training, and doing things together – such as building, or taking part in everyday activities.

This kind of research necessarily changes your relationship with the people with whom you are working. Some control must be relinquished, but this should not relegate you to neutral facilitator. Instead, it is important to consider yourself an active participant with certain knowledge and proficiencies, who is also present to learn and be altered by the process. Peer learning has a strong social dimension, and can help you form new relationships and strengthen existing ones. Learning enables a more effective critique of existing situations and, as a greater number of people are empowered, far more sophisticated and nuanced engagement with issues and concerns.

The benefits for your practice of doing this successfully are clear: the legacy of a project goes beyond the physical aspects of a scheme, and as an active participant you are developing skills and proficiencies beyond those that may be taught in architectural schools, or as part of CPD programmes. It could also be argued that it is only through learning together that meaningful and transformative change will occur. In the 1980s, feminist design cooperative Matrix (including Anne Thorne of Anne Thorne Architects, featured in this book) were pioneering in raising issues from procurement to building techniques, and they supported learning through the production of publications and technical advice, particularly in relation to women and their experiences of using and making the built environment. Their impact as a practice is expressed through raising awareness and developing a better understanding of important social and political issues in the architectural community.

Co-design and proposing alternatives

Co-design emphasises the whole of a design process, from inception through to realisation and use – opportunities for creative involvement should be offered throughout. Design is an iterative process, and designing with others requires that the decision-making is something that all participants can understand and actively engage with. Through helping the client and user groups to understand aspects such as statutory obligations, material selection, budgeting and construction techniques, practices can become effective in their involvement in a project and understand restrictions that bear upon the design and construction teams. Visualisations that are incomplete or more tentative can allow space for people to add their layer or response.

Testing things in the place for which they are conceived through building temporary structures or intervening 'on site' can enable this process to be rigorous and accessible to a broad group. In this way people can get involved for a short period of time and still make a useful contribution to your research – responding in ways that are framed by their experiences and how space is used, rather than a limited number of design options or their preconceptions of what might be expected of them. By rigorously recording and reflecting on the questions and ways of working that come from these processes (ideally with those who took part) this work can inform future practice. Art and architecture practices such as Public Works[12] and Studio Polpo often work in such ways, emphasising architecture as something processual that changes relations, above its manifestation as artefact.

Critiquing received notions and reflecting on your role[13]

Through conducting post-occupancy evaluations,[14] exhibitions and case studies, it is possible to question received notions about what makes a project a success. This could be done through participant and non-participant observation, interviews and mapping. By gathering and combining quantitative and qualitative information, a picture can be formed of how a place responds to change over time, and what the opportunities are for modifying the design or refining future proposals. These methods can bring together potentially hidden (or absent) voices and opinions, through foregrounding experiences and knowledge of those using a building or place. It is important that these critiques are shared visibly, to allow for debate and conversation; often this is about making something that was considered to be an economic or social issue into a political one, where people and concerns are heard publicly.

SUMMARY

All of these research elements and methods contribute to the development of your ethical and philosophical position as an architect. These explorations can clarify and exemplify where you stand on issues such as sustainability, equity, gentrification, participation and extending access to architectural and design services. Research offers a space to explore and reflect on how different methods produce different kinds of architecture, and empower people to change the city in ways that matter to them.

1 For example see BDR's use of mapping in a wider storytelling process, as discussed in Prue Chiles' 'What if...?; a narrative process for re-imagining the city', in P. Blundell Jones, D. Petrescu & J. Till, eds. (2013), *Architecture and Participation* (Abingdon: Routledge) Chapter 14, pp. 197–206.

2 1980s feminist cooperative design practice Matrix published their work in order to raise awareness of women's issues in the built environment and the architectural and building professions. See: Matrix (1984), *Making Space: Women and the Man-Made Environment* (London: Pluto Press) and Matrix (1986), *A Job Designing Buildings: For Women Interested in Architecture and Buildings* (London: Matrix Feminist Design Co-operative).

3 For good critical analyses of participatory action research, see: R. Pain & P. Francis (2003) 'Reflections on Participatory Research' *Area*, **35**, pp. 46–57; J. McNiff & J. Whitehead (2002), *Action Research: Principles and Practice* (London: Routledge); W.F.E. Whyte (1991), *Participatory Action Research* (London: Sage).

4 Community Design Centres, which provided architectural services at neighbourhood level in the US, are a good example of these kinds of approaches. German architectural magazine *Anarchitektur* has three special issues on their development, which are useful for developing practice. See: O. Clemens, J. Fezer & S. Horlitz, eds., 'Community Design: Involvement and Architecture in the US since 1963', *Anarchitektur* (2008).

5 The ethics and motivations for cooperative approaches to research are explored in J. Heron & P. Reason's 'The Practice of Co-operative Inquiry: Research "With" Rather Than "On" People' in P. Reason & H. Bradbury (2006), *Handbook of Action Research* (London: Sage), pp. 144–54.

6 See: H. Lefebvre, trans. by D. Nicholson-Smith (1991), *The Production of Space* (Oxford: Blackwell); 'The Right to the City' in H. Lefebvre, trans. by E. Kofman & E. Lebas (1996), *Writings On Cities* (Oxford: Blackwell), pp. 63–181.

   Lefebvre was incredibly influential, for example on the Situationist International group (see for example S. Sadler (1998) *The Situationist City* (Cambridge, MA: MIT Press)), and David Harvey (see for example D. Harvey (2012), *Rebel Cities: From the Right to the City to the Urban Revolution* (London: Verso Books).

7 See Anna Holder's work around initiating architectural projects: A. Holder (2014), *Initiating Architecture: Agency, Knowledge and Values in Instigating Spatial Change* (University of Sheffield: PhD thesis).

8 For example, see University of Sheffield School of Architecture (n.d.), *Research Ethics and Integrity* (University of Sheffield: www.sheffield.ac.uk/architecture/research/ethics).

9 See, for example C. Puthod, *et al.* (2000), *Creative Spaces: A Toolkit for Participatory Urban Design* (London: Architecture Foundation).

10 See the work of Architect Doina Petrescu, especially: D. Petrescu (2007), *How to Make a Community as Well as the Space for It* (Republic: seminaire.samizdat.net/IMG/pdf/Doina_Petrescu_-2.pdf).

11 For example see Puthod, *Creative Space.*

12   For example Public Works Serpentine Pavilion project documented by K.
      Böhm in Public Works (2006), *If you can't find it, give us a ring* (ARTicle Press:
      www.publicworksgroup.net/publications/if-you-cant-find-itgive-us-a-ring).

13   See: D. Schön (1983), *The Reflective Practitioner: How Practitioners Think in Action*
      (New York: Basic Books).

14   For example, see the work of Cooper Marcus, including C. Marcus & C. & C. Francis
      'Post Occupancy Evaluation' in L. Hopper, ed. (2006), *Landscape Architectural Graphic
      Standards* (New York: Wiley).

DEMYSTIFYING ARCHITECTURAL RESEARCH

Chapter 9

EDUCATION AND ENGAGEMENT

RICHARD COTTRELL, COTTRELL & VERMEULEN ARCHITECTURE

CONTRIBUTOR PROFILE: RICHARD COTTRELL
Richard Cottrell co-founded Cottrell & Vermeulen Architecture with Brian Vermeulen in 1992. As well as his own practice he is a studio tutor at the Cass School of Architecture at London Metropolitan University.

M any of our built projects to date have been educational buildings and schools. Aside from our interest in designing environments that enable and encourage learning, we have increasingly found that schools are among the few remaining places in our society where communities come together.

Practice profile: Cottrell & Vermeulen Architects

Cottrell and Vermeulen Architects was founded in 1992, and is a small to medium practice of 18, based in London. They work primarily on education, community, housing, health, arts, residential, landscape and master-planning projects.

The practice views its buildings as the result of a dialogue between practice and research. They view even small-scale projects as having a significant impact on the local community, and as having the potential to catalyse renewal and regeneration in the wider neighbourhood. An example is their ongoing research into school design which is largely conducted through community engagement, and also draws on experiences from previous projects, leading to bespoke design solutions.

CONTEXT

In 2003 we contributed to the Department for Education and Skills publication *Building Schools for the Future*.[1] Using the specific knowledge of learning environments that we had gained from practice, we formulated concepts and ideas for an exemplar primary school design. Following on from that, the studio has developed a variety of pedagogical briefs including a vocational college, a high street academy and a middle school. These speculative projects allow us to consider how schools can relate to the city and the public realm and speculate on how school typologies might be redefined.

As part of our teaching methodology we initiate workshops with local schools to provide a specific context in which to test a more abstract discourse. The Peckham experiment, for example, proposed a middle school on a dense urban site that created new connections between younger and older children, neighbouring schools and local communities. The design of threshold conditions was critical to our research, and we considered typologies of edge building and transition space – gatehouses, arcades and foyers – to integrate schools into the urban fabric. During the year the studio collaborated with Lyndhurst Primary School through a series of workshops with pupils. Simultaneously, as a practice we were developing an expansion strategy for the school through Southwark's Primary Capital framework.

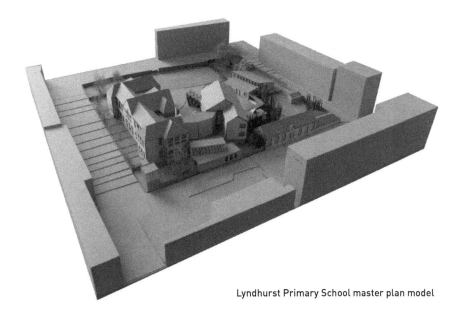

Lyndhurst Primary School master plan model

APPROACH

Philosophy
In practice we have found that when working within the constraints of framework commissions the schools themselves are distanced from the design process. Coupled with this inflexible and top-down generic approach, the strictures of contractor-led procurement exclude meaningful client and community engagement. It is only through instigating workshops – beyond the standardised methodology of these projects – that we are able to engage schools in the creative process. Critical to our work is the assertion that, in order for school design to flourish, it is essential that the school community participates actively with design and decision-making.

Methods
At Lyndhurst our teaching studio collaborated with Year 6 pupils to produce collage models of an imagined landscape for learning. Through the process of talking and making, unexpected and speculative proposals emerged which were populated with a treehouse, bandstand, radio station and new school entrance. In our experience, working with collage techniques and sketch models is an effective way for pupils of different ages to communicate relevant knowledge and an in-depth understanding of their school environment. Specifically, by engaging pupils in making, the process can reveal sophisticated ideas and insightful speculations.

INSIGHTS AND IMPACT

The collage models from the workshop were developed in the studio, and collected into a group model. The process and the resulting model were presented to the pupils, staff, parents and other stakeholders at the school. The ensuing conversations provided an opportunity to engage in conversations about the wider context of the expansion strategy, which had been informed by the workshop. The subsequent dialogue was based on the ideas, imagination and creativity of the school, and we were able to explicitly demonstrate our willingness to listen and respond to the school community.

Furthermore our findings influenced how, as a studio, we approached the strategic scale of the Peckham Experiment brief, by understanding local and specific issues. The studio's middle school proposals were presented to Southwark in the context of the Department for Education's current Primary Capital programme and suggested tangible ways to transform the structure and topography of compulsory education in the borough.

LESSONS

In practice we continue to maintain that our architecture should be a response to a specific context and its local community. As we increasingly find that projects are subject to generic and standardised constraints, our research and our involvement with education proves a valuable means to practise this ethos, and to engage with the people who use our buildings.

We contend that consultation can be a creative part of the design process rather than a series of boxes to tick. Through recent teaching studio projects we have been able to engage in conversations with clients, policymakers and commissioning bodies, using a different tone than would be possible in practice. Finally, as Cottrell and Vermeulen Architects continues to practice in Southwark, our studio helps us to sustain a meaningful dialogue with the communities who inform and inspire the buildings that we build, and the places that we make.

---

1   Department for Education and Skills (2004) *Building Schools for the Future* page 70 (DfES, 2004: www.education.gov.uk/publications/eOrderingDownload/DfES%200134%20 200MIG469.pdf).

Chapter 10

CO-DESIGN FOR NEW LIFESTYLES

JANE BURNSIDE, JANE D BURNSIDE ARCHITECTS

CONTRIBUTOR PROFILE: JANE BURNSIDE
Jane Burnside is Principal of Jane D Burnside Architects. As well as publishing widely, she has also had roles advising the Northern Ireland Assembly on Rural Planning Policy reform and as a lecturer at Queen's University, Belfast. Jane is also a former Rome Scholar in Architecture.

The houses we design should reflect the lifestyles that exist today, and there are as many different designs for contemporary houses as there are contemporary lifestyles. However, not all designers know how to read their clients, and not all clients know how to communicate their lifestyle needs to the designer. Although housebuilding has been popularised in the media, the actual process of design – that of communication and decision-making, moving from complexity to an artful simplicity that really takes into account client needs and desires – is rarely mentioned.

So while architects must recognise and respond to changing lifestyles, the public needs to be empowered with enough knowledge of the design process to help both to achieve the best possible design. I try to enable this through a rigorous consultation process that I have refined and reflected on through my writings.

Practice profile: Jane D Burnside Architects
Founded in 1993, Jane D Burnside Architects is a micro-practice specialising in rural housing and rural planning. The practice is based in Kells, County Antrim, and Tobermory on the Isle of Mull.

While the practice's intention in doing research is to create a business advantage – setting itself apart from competing practices – it also reflects an interest in societal change, and architecture that is both grounded in place and in clients' ongoing personal histories, explored through design.[2]

CONTEXT

Building one-off houses in the open countryside is permitted in Northern Ireland. While one might think this would present a golden opportunity for architectural expression, when I started in practice few new rural houses ever saw the hand of an architect – the profession was not interested. Instead, the public sought assistance from plan drawers who reproduced their stock of mock Georgian bungalows which were then stamped in series across the countryside.

APPROACH

Philosophy
Architects should not strive to design the 'perfect' contemporary house; rather we need to design contemporary houses that reflect various contemporary lifestyle needs. To that end, the architect needs to get inside the client's head. This requires more listening and less speaking, behaving more like a therapist and less like a theorist!

Methods

There are three elements to the engagement process: vision, identity and context. Determining a client's priorities within this framework requires active listening and questioning as well as an ability to detach oneself from one's own ideas and preferences – a method somewhat akin to some interview methods in the social sciences[3] – while site analysis uses other more graphical skills from the architect's canon.

The vision

Imagine that you are at a dinner party where, instead of a name-card at your place setting, everyone has a cardboard cut-out of their house. What do you think the cut-outs might tell you about the people you are talking to? Would it make a difference to your impression of them?

Where we choose to live says something about our life's vision, to some degree. So, how do we access a private view of our client's personal vision?

Mood boards are usually prepared by designers who present their ideas to their clients. I reverse this by getting clients to prepare a mood board of images they love. Enabling clients to get in touch with what they really want from their new home helps me to understand what I need to achieve for them.

While mood boards address the heart, the brief addresses facts. There are two key parts to the brief: a schedule of accommodation and the client's unique requirements. Though the former is a tangible list of physical spaces, the latter is about getting clients to consider how they will actually use their physical space on a daily basis; the aim is to understand how the clients actually *will* live, not how they might think they would *like* to live.

The identity

Although there could be as many different contemporary houses as there are contemporary lifestyles, similar design issues recur for similar groups of people. So we need to face the challenge of designing contemporary houses that reflect the various lifestyles of their occupants – the solo woman or man, different sorts of families, and retirees. The first challenge is to acknowledge that new groups that are emerging. For example, over a quarter of all US households were living alone in 2011, totalling 33 million Americans.[4] New York University's Professor Eric Klinenberg claims that 'solitary living is the biggest social change that we have neglected to identify, let alone examine'.[5] A similar trend is emerging in the UK,[6] with other growth groups including blended families and retirees. We need to respond to the challenge by designing contemporary houses that respond to these contemporary lifestyles.

For example, some solo women do not want, in their homes, overtones of male dominance. Other women, who have perhaps experienced divorce, want their homes to feel secure. Still others, who have chosen not to have a family themselves nevertheless want their home to embrace a large extended family; a home for solo living may also need to accommodate large numbers of people.

Designing for the solo man presents different challenges to designing for the solo woman. Some men are concerned with the impression their home makes on other people – perhaps more so than some women. To really work it should be an honest expression of who the client is, and his particular brand of masculinity.

Today families come in all shapes and sizes, including blended families. With separation or divorce, families become more complex, and homes should reflect these changing dynamics.

Finally, our growing population of retirees often have a pioneering spirit – perhaps stimulated by the prospect of a new beginning – and this often brings forth the desire for a new home. Longer periods of indoor living mean that a sense of space and good-quality natural light – along with design for accessibility – becomes a priority.

The context

When a house is in the countryside you are adding a permanent object to a natural landscape shared by others – a sobering thought. Success lies in engaging clients with their site from the outset. I always start by finding a spot where we most enjoy standing – and take the clients through a process of imagining which room of the house they would like to be in at that moment in space and time. If a client feels uncomfortable on the top of a hill, it is unlikely they will feel differently if their house is built there.

Discussing the approach to the house can be very revealing. Approaches can be frontal, oblique or spiral; compressed into a short distance or expanded over hundreds of metres. The frontal approach is the architectural equivalent of a trumpet fanfare: not for the shy or faint-hearted. Oblique and spiralling approaches are best suited to those with a more carefree outlook, or an instinctive curiosity for life.

Discussing a client's mood board eventually
an overall sense of the new building emerges

INSIGHTS AND IMPACT

By developing practice expertise – such as the approaches to vision, identity and context in contemporary rural house design – I achieve more commissions than I would otherwise. But what I am most proud of is that I have raised the level of expectation in rural housing design, empowering the public to demand better buildings from their architects and agents.

LESSONS

For me, becoming an expert was fuelled by a passion to promote better buildings in our landscape: raising the design bar with a consistent vision; reforming government planning policy to include a focus on design and empowering clients through my book *Contemporary Design Secrets: the Art of Building a House in the Countryside* so they can demand better buildings for themselves. Other architects wanting to follow a similar path must realise that having a media presence is all-important; I have written hundreds of articles for magazines and newspapers showcasing my work and debating the issues related to rural planning – people keep them, and they appear from behind the mantle clock years later when they commission me! Having a rigorous intellectual foundation for these articles is important in communicating authority on the subject, as well as professionalism.

---

1   Including: Jane Burnside (2013), *Contemporary Design Secrets: the Art of Building a House in the Countryside* (Dublin: Booklink).

2   Design research has been described as 'a confluence of architecture, history, storytelling and landscaping'. M. Fraser (2013), *Design Research in Architecture: An Overview* (Farnham: Ashgate).

3   For example, interview data can be used in Grounded Theory methodology, where theory is derived from the data and where the development of theory has a close relationship with the gathering and analysis of the data. See A. Strauss & J. Corbin (1998), *Basics of Qualitative Research* 2nd ed. (London: Sage).

4   E. Klinenberg (2012), 'Living Alone is the New Norm' *TIME*, **179**(10).

5   *Ibid*

6   DCLG (2013), Household Interim Projections, 2011 to 2021, England (UK Government: www.gov.uk).

Chapter 11

VISIONING BRENTFORD LOCK WEST

JOHN SAMPSON, URBED

CONTRIBUTOR PROFILE: JOHN SAMPSON
John Sampson is an urban designer and architect at URBED with over ten years' professional experience. He has collaborated on a number of action research projects,[1] ranging from developing community-led design solutions for low-carbon neighbourhoods through to best-practice guidance on parking provision.

O ver a number of years the practice has invested in 'design for change',[2] an engagement methodology aimed at allowing tenants to actively and meaningfully engage, communicate and co-design with architects. The process was originally developed out of URBED's involvement with the Homes for Change housing cooperative in Manchester. We were later commissioned to formalise the process into a training course for the charity The Glass-House.

This has led to further opportunities to test and develop our engagement methodology. In recent years the most interesting opportunity to do this came from Brentford Lock West, where we were commissioned, based on our experience working with local communities, to co-design a scheme with a resistant local community.

Practice profile: URBED
Founded in 1975 and based in Manchester, URBED (URBanism, Environment and Design) is a small employee-owned cooperative. The practice has ten staff and associates, including urban planners, architects, an economist and a sustainability expert. The practice works in three main areas:

1. Public-sector consultancy
2. Master planning for developers and housebuilders
3. Research, writing and advocacy, including policy reports for government, research for think tanks, and in-house publications and events

The practice undertakes research activities for two main reasons: first because of the pleasure that research – learning new things – brings and second because it has a history of bringing new work to the office. The practice uses knowledge and understanding gained from research to prepare them to work in a new field; it also helps them to target and develop new markets.

CONTEXT

Brentford Lock West is situated on the edge of Brentford town centre. The area is currently in a state of transition spearheaded by the local community, who vigorously and successfully campaigned against a previous high-density residential development on the site back in 2004. Following the planning refusal the client, ISIS Waterside Regeneration Ltd (then part of the Igloo Regeneration Fund group), organised a competition to appoint a new design team. Their brief set out an aspiration to develop an exemplar sustainable neighbourhood that would successfully integrate family housing into a viable scheme that celebrated the qualities of Brentford.

Following the design competition two of the entrants were asked to collaborate, and so a design team was formed consisting of URBED, Tovatt Architects & Planners, and Swedish master planner Klas Tham. Over the next 18 months of intensive involvement by ISIS and URBED the scheme was transformed into one that supported the regeneration of the town and had the broad support of the community.

APPROACH

Philosophy
URBED have a strong interest in engaging local people in the design process, which has led to the development of techniques such as 'design for change', used for the Brentford Lock West project.

Methods
The design process was one of collaboration with the local community. This started with workshops run over two evenings at the start of the process in a local cafe. Residents and stakeholders from the area used the first session to develop a shared understanding of the area today. The second evening focused on generating a number of different options for the site, using collage and plasticine models.

These models were then drawn up by the design team and presented back to the community at a public consultation event to help the design team focus on a preferred development framework. Following feedback from this event, an emerging development framework was drawn up. This was then tested and developed further by the design team, and shared with the community through regular update events and exhibitions. In total seven engagement events were held, in addition to which ISIS regularly presented progress to local boards and panels throughout the 18 months it took to develop the scheme. Findings from the research were published on the URBED website,[3] and formed part of the planning application for the development.

INSIGHTS AND IMPACT

This process was essential in re-engaging a previously mistrustful local community, and many of the people who participated in the design workshops had been actively involved in the campaign against the previous application. The scheme that embodied the findings from the consultation process was granted outline planning in March 2011. The planning committee praised ISIS for their meaningful involvement of the local community in the development process, something that is a model for developer-led engagement under the localism agenda.

Before commencing the public engagement we were aware that it was essential that the expectations of both the community and the developer were clearly established at each stage of the process. In running design workshops it was important that ISIS took on board the comments of the local residents, while the community acknowledged ISIS's need as a developer to design a commercially viable project. With these criteria clearly set out, the engagement process resulted in a scheme that the local community feels a sense of ownership over. With localism becoming more embedded within the planning system, this project demonstrates that community engagement can be beneficial for both the client and the local community.

LESSONS

A number of lessons came from the project, which will inform the practice's future work:

- Working so closely and intensively with the residents who had originally opposed the scheme meant that we were able to understand their concerns and aspirations. At the same time the residents were able to gain a greater understanding of the developer's requirements for the site. Building this kind of joint understanding takes time and resources. The value created through this process far outweighs the additional cost to the client of undertaking this additional engagement.
- Developing the 'design for change' methodology as a tool has provided us with a tangible asset that we can market.
- Finally, the success of Brentford Lock West has led to significant further commissions by Igloo to work on sites across the country.

Designing in public: engaged local residents in
Brentford analysing the local area as part of the
'design for change' process

1   Action research is a process in which the subject of the research is relevant to the practitioners and, importantly, where taking informed action on the basis of the findings is an integral part of the research process. It is often used in the education field, but has direct relevance to the practice of architecture. There are a number of accessible introductions to action research freely available on the web, for example;

Infed.org (2007), *Action Research* (infed.org: infed.org/mobi/action-research).

O'Brien 'Um exame da abordagem metodológica da pesquisa ação [An Overview of the Methodological Approach of Action Research]' in Roberto Richardson, ed. (1998), *Teoria e Prática da Pesquisa Ação [Theory and Practice of Action Research]* (Universidade Federal da Paraíba: João Pessoa, Brazil). English version available at www.web.ca/~robrien/papers/arfinal.html

2   A workshop-based methodology related to action research and co-design; another reflective research methodology. See D. Rudlin & N. Falk (1999), *Sustainable Urban Neighbourhood: Building the 21st Century Home* (Oxford: Architectural Press), p. 238.

3   URBED, Tovatt Architects & Planners, and Klas Tham (2009) *Design for Change Event – Brentford Workshop Outcomes* (URBED: urbed.coop/projects/brentford-lock-west).

Chapter 12

EXPERIMENTAL RESIDENTIAL

MARK PARSONS, STUDIO POLPO

CONTRIBUTOR PROFILE: MARK PARSONS
Mark Parsons is an architect and co-founder of Studio Polpo. He has worked in a number of practices, most recently Architype (from 2002), with whom he continues to collaborate. Mark has taught at the University of Sheffield School of Architecture on both degree and master's courses since 2005.

Experimental Residential was a piece of research that came out of a 'failed' project (the client was unable to source funding). Studio Polpo had been asked to put together a feasibility proposal for the reuse of an empty commercial building as a short-term live-work space for the Common People community interest company (CIC) – an organisation primarily involved in pop-up shops and events in the city.

We suggested to Common People that – in order to overcome their funding problem – support might be available for the project if the feasibility work they required were documented in such a way that it could be disseminated, forming a useful document for other groups considering similar projects. In the first instance research was used as an 'initiating tool'[1] which connected critical and theoretical knowledge with a live, prototypical and exploratory project.

Practice profile: Studio Polpo

Studio Polpo is a Sheffield-based micro architecture practice (six people) set up as a social enterprise, which works primarily with the third sector. The practice works collaboratively – with a range of organisations and individuals – at various scales, from bespoke furniture to buildings.

The practice uses research as a mechanism for exploring new ideas; research is either driven by a project-specific issue or an issue of interest to the practice. They approach research as a way of creating a space in which to test ideas that allows for failure or unexpected results. The practice also uses research methods to collate, analyse and summarise knowledge from others, which they then disseminate – for example online.[2]

CONTEXT

The city of Sheffield has a large number of empty commercial and industrial buildings in its centre, many of which are of little architectural significance by themselves, but which form the layers of history that give the city its character. The city council has been keen to address the issue of these – often prominent – empty spaces.

We have undertaken a number of projects and collaborations which demonstrate how these types of building can be adapted or inhabited. One example is the ongoing OPERA series of pop-up houses,[3] which use performance to reintroduce residential activity into unused buildings. As a result of the project we were approached by Common People, who were keen to explore how empty buildings could be used as short-term places to live.

Common People had identified 121 Eyre Street, Sheffield (a mid-twentieth-century former funeral parlour and college) as a building that could be used as a large shared house. The building has solid brick walls and single glazing, and had only recently been vacated, leaving it in a good state of repair. The desire was to explore how to create a cooperative model for a shared house and work space, both in terms of organisational (rental and governance) and building (fire strategy, heat loss and planning) terms.

APPROACH

Philosophy

All of our projects – including our research projects – are underpinned by our desire to work towards social, environmental and economic sustainability. These aims led us to set up our practice as a social enterprise, where profits are reinvested in the business or in the community.

We are interested in influencing, intervening and changing how things are done. We also want to support others striving to do good things, and we use part of our profits to invest in new initiatives and help get projects off the ground. Most of our work is in collaboration with others – we believe that engaging with people from different disciplines and backgrounds makes our work more interesting.

Methods

As the client could not fund feasibility work, we suggested that we apply for funding and, if successful, use this to pay for research and design work, but also for documentation and dissemination, so that whatever the eventual outcome of the Eyre Street project there would be a publicly (and freely) available piece of work that could inform others and, we hoped, make a difference in the city. We secured funding from Innovate UK, but then learned from the client that – for legal reasons – the building could not be used as anticipated.

This changed the emphasis of the project from a site-specific focus to a more general one. We decided to concentrate more on collecting and analysing relevant case studies, instigating roundtable discussions with planners, housing officers and developers to explore and understand policy and the barriers/ opportunities associated with reuse of these building types; as well as prototyping and testing (including thermal testing) a demountable and low-cost secondary glazing system, for which a need had been identified on similar projects. For the latter we worked with acoustic specialists from the University of Sheffield, as well as building on previous student work.[4] The findings have been made available in both digital[5] and newspaper formats to achieve maximum reach.

INSIGHTS AND IMPACT

The most straightforward outcomes for the practice have been from our research into the rules, laws and issues related to planning and building use – primarily around rates versus Council Tax, and the way in which temporary use planning works – that have increased our knowledge base. Our discussions with diverse council officers and organisations working with empty buildings have both opened up new avenues of work for the practice and highlighted grey areas within the planning system, which we are seeking to understand further – for example it appears that it may not actually be illegal to inhabit spaces without change of use.

The secondary glazing prototype has generated interest from two organisations interested in using it, and further development and installation of this has been built into a funding bid by another client. Although currently open source – to allow uptake and development – this is potentially a system that could become a start-up business in itself.

For the client, as a company initiating temporary use strategies in the city, Common People now have a publication associated with them that will help them to gain publicity. Most importantly, through sharing this material and taking advantage of the client's networks and contacts, we are not only raising the practice's profile but (we believe) putting important research – which would otherwise remain within academia – into the public realm where it can be used.

LESSONS

We believe that freely sharing knowledge (while being clearly associated with its production) is crucial to allowing others to usefully build on what has been done before. For example, we have been invited to share details about Experimental Residential at two recent housing conferences (which has also led to new contacts and opportunities for the practice).

There is often no time or space for reflection, testing or research in practice. Applying for funding with clients or other bodies is a very useful way of securing both time and a structure to allow research to happen outside of normal project pressures. Engaging people from outside the practice to assist with research projects can also bring a valuable external perspective; one example of this is our recent collaboration with a filmmaker as part of the OPERA projects. Finally, we believe that research should be integral to prototyping – not just of products, but also approaches, strategies and local government policy.

Prototype of secondary glazing joint

1   A. Holder (2014), *Initiating Architecture: Agency, Knowledge and Values in Instigating Spatial Change* (University of Sheffield: PhD thesis).

2   www.studiopolpo.com

3   Studio Polpo (2014) OPERA #1 (Studio Polpo: www.studiopolpo.com)

    Studio Polpo (2015) Blog: *OPERA #2 starts on Sunday 22 March* (Studio Polpo: www.studiopolpo.com).

4   Live Projects (2014) One Great Workshop (University of Sheffield: www.liveprojects.org).

    One Great Workshop (2014–) Blog: *One Great Workshop* (University of Sheffield: onegreatworkshop.wordpress.com).

5   Studio Polpo (2015) *Common Rooms* (Studio Polpo: www.studiopolpo.com).

Chapter 13

BRIDGING THERMAL INEQUALITY IN GLASGOW

RUPERT DALY, COLLECTIVE ARCHITECTURE

CONTRIBUTOR PROFILE: RUPERT DALY
Rupert Daly is an architect at Collective Architecture specialising in sustainable design, low-carbon techniques and modern methods of construction. He has led a series of large-scale housing projects for housing association and care providers as well as a number of renovation projects within traditional buildings. Rupert is a certified Passive House Designer.

The Cedar Flats research project – carried out in close collaboration with our client Queens Cross Housing Association – explored the viability of retaining a series of three 1960s tower blocks in Glasgow's West End, and whether these might be refurbished to Passive House standards.

Practice profile: Collective Architecture

Collective Architecture is a Glasgow-based cooperative large–medium design studio with 28 staff. The practice works on commercial, community, conservation, cultural, health, lighting, master planning and residential projects.

The practice's interest in research mirrors their interest in the built environment. Their investigations include socio-political constructs, physical and non-physical infrastructure, methods of construction, alleviation of fuel poverty and community engagement. They view their research as part of a wider exploration of the way in which towns and cities are formed, and as a way of understanding the cultural landscape in which they create. They believe that their research informs and improves their work – the physical practice of architecture.

CONTEXT

In April 2011 Queens Cross Housing Association successfully gained the vote of local people to become the registered social landlord of the Woodside neighbourhood. They established the Woodside Community Involvement Group, comprising local people from a variety of cultures.

In 2013 Collective Architecture worked with the Association and Community Group to carry out a feasibility study that investigated opportunities for the existing housing stock and open spaces. The housing typologies ranged from four-storey brick deck-access flats to high-rise tower blocks. Through extensive community consultation and engagement, local people identified a range of issues that affected them. These included recycling and refuse, access and security, building fabric, communal areas and facilities, external environment including green space, growing space, and soft landscapes.

The study investigated options for both demolition and retention of three dominant tower blocks – the Cedar Flats. The outcome of the study, and intensive consultation with residents within the towers was that the tower blocks should be retained. They were to be refurbished to improve their energy performance and enhance the quality of both communal areas and individual flats for all residents.

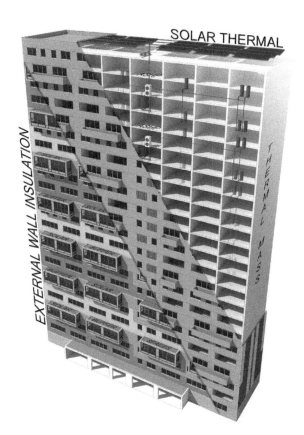

SOLAR THERMAL

EXTERNAL WALL INSULATION

THERMAL MASS

APPROACH

Philosophy

The Cedar Flats project forms a 'meeting of minds' between architect and client. The primary aim for the Association was to reduce fuel poverty for approximately 800 local residents. The team were conscious that Passive House principles in Scotland had principally been applied to one-off homes for people with higher socio-economic status (primarily in rural areas). They therefore aimed to apply the Passive House principles to address energy consumption for as many people as possible in an urban context.

The team worked together to push the boundaries of a 'fabric first' approach (within high-rise tower refurbishment) and to advance their work to a higher level of performance than they had delivered on previous projects. The project also sought to make significant environmental improvements in relation to air quality, comfort levels and shared amenity.

Methods
The architect, client and M&E (mechanical and electrical) engineer conducted a series of feasibility performance specifications for a number of energy sources such as biomass and ground-source heat pumps. These were then tested against a 'fabric first' Passive House approach. These were both measured relative to one another in terms of build cost, life cycle costing and funding opportunities in relation to the reduced energy costs for the residents. The principal tool for this high-level study was the Passive House Planning Package.

INSIGHTS AND IMPACT

The compact form of the building typology and construction type gave us a great starting point for a very efficient thermal envelope and achievable high levels of airtightness. We carried out significant research into the performance of various mechanical ventilation heat recovery (MVHR) systems currently available, as well as more recent product innovations which work on a decentralised, demand-controlled ventilation and heat recovery basis. The more recent innovations are a potential industry game changer, reducing maintenance, running costs and overall project cost while providing good air quality and comfort levels.

The project findings have been disseminated via the following channels:

- Review meetings with other housing associations
- Presentation to the Scottish Ecological Design Association (SEDA)
- Evaluation of the project via the Mackintosh Environmental Architecture Research Unit (MEARU) – before, during and after completion

The project benefits Collective Architecture in a number of ways. First, it ensures that our practice remains at the forefront of sustainable design and development. Second, we can continue to practically address both physical and social aspects of architecture and the built environment. Third, it allowed me to apply my specialist training and skills in Passive House technology to an ambitious and significant project in Glasgow's city centre. From a business perspective, the project offered us the opportunity to 'lead the way' in terms of how city councils and large-scale housing providers might address fuel poverty and residential refurbishment using twenty-first-century thinking and technology.

LESSONS

Having a live project to apply research to had a significant impact on the learning outcomes. The research element of this project has helped change our perception of how and when research should be conducted, as well as benefiting all stakeholders.

Early engagement is key, as is allocating a fee for the extra work involved. Ultimately there should be a win-win situation for the client and all those involved. The funding element ensures that the research is perpetual for the practice and it is a conscious decision for the practice to ensure this is allocated.

We are actively discussing projects at a strategic level to facilitate innovation. Our view is that research should be a partnership between academics, business, industry and the public sector. Evidence-based research can be invaluable in securing the success of a project as well as opening doors to other funding opportunities and business growth. It enables us to inform the decision-making process and facilitate innovation.

Part 3
Cultural Research Practice

Chapter 14

DEMYSTIFYING CULTURAL RESEARCH METHODS

STEPHEN WALKER, UNIVERSITY OF SHEFFIELD

CONTRIBUTOR PROFILE: STEPHEN WALKER
Stephen Walker is a Reader in Architecture at the University of Sheffield. His research takes place on the peripheries of architecture, involving contemporary arts practice and critical theory, working with a range of subjects from medieval Breton architecture to contemporary ring roads, artists and temporary fairgrounds, and much in between.

CONTEXT

What, or who, is this cultural architect? Haven't architects always been closely associated with cultural production? Contemporary interest in 'culture' has seen some practitioners expand their repertoire, explicitly increasing the range of their activities, adapting the organisation of their practices, and widening the scope of work they produce. Architectural practices are increasingly comfortable and adept at understanding the cultural value, or *cultural capital*, they generate. The cultural capital of some so-called starchitects is exploited by and for clients around the globe, who believe that they (or their organisation, their city or their region) will benefit from a building that bears a recognisable architectural signature. But cultural value should not be reduced to this single mode of production.

Without getting bogged down in too much history, it is worth recalling some of the broadest architectural trends of the twentieth century, as this helps to contextualise and explain the emergence of today's cultural architect. Mounting a challenge to the functional, rationalist approach to architecture – which arguably dominated architectural practice and culture from the start of the twentieth century (when an increasing dominance of scientific method was sufficient motivation for many architects and artists to attempt to demonstrate scientific consistency and universal principles within their own disciplines) – the cultural architect now arguably takes up a much greater number of roles and approaches.

Architectural cultural production was for much of the twentieth century underwritten by a belief in the disciplinary purity of practice. This peaked in the post-war period and was increasingly challenged (from various directions) from the 1960s onwards. Effects were widespread, witnessed in art and architectural practice, theatre, ethnography and politics. Within the academic world, perhaps the most significant manifestation was the establishment of Cultural Studies – an actively interdisciplinary and inclusive intellectual movement – in the 1970s by influential thinkers such as Raymond Williams.[1]

The influence of Cultural Studies (and the methods related to it) as a way of thinking and looking has been broad and multifaceted, extending to material and symbolic cultures. To focus this discussion about cultural research methods it is useful to consider the impact of Cultural Studies on approaches that some architectural practices are now taking to their work.

CULTURAL APPROACHES AND METHODS

Case studies

Andrea Kahn has encouraged architects to approach site as a 'thick concept'[2] – they should go beyond more easily measured and recorded physical properties in order to understand the influence (and importance) of a wider range of characteristics and phenomena that contribute to experience of site. In *Site Matters*,[3] Burns and Kahn identify several constructs of site that can provoke and promote the work of the cultural architect in equal measure, including site as: 'relational construct', 'socially constructed', 'experimental/material construct', 'historiographical construct', 'as construct of analysis techniques' and of 'modes of representation'. Much of the impetus for the broadening of approach that Kahn's work represents can be found in what Rosalind Krauss has referred to as the 'Expanded Field',[4] which challenged the narrow definitions of architecture and sculpture which circulated in the post-war years.

This can be linked to case study methodologies from OS31 (Tony Broomhead) and Helen Stratford. In different ways, their work seeks to develop a 'thick' understanding of site by using arts-based practices such as filmmaking and conversation. These methods increase the kinds of information architects have to work with when responding to a site with design proposals.

In the case of OS31's Square Routes, a small group of young people worked with the practice over relatively short sessions, making and then showcasing videos that give voice to a significant group of users that would frequently be invisible in the survey and briefing process. The most challenging aspect of using these types of methods can be finding a willing group of participants. However, equipment is easy to provide – as videos taken on most smartphones can be of good quality – and video-editing software is widely available as freeware or at little cost.

OS31 are clear that this approach is neither token 'participation' nor a radical shift in architectural practice; what it does provide the architects with is a broader appreciation of social constructions that relate to a particular site, and a ground-level, mobile view of the site as produced and valued by this group. As a by-product perhaps, it also generates interest and involvement in the place or project within a demographic that is usually disenfranchised from the procurement of most building projects.

Helen Stratford worked on Market Meditations not as a project architect, but as a cultural agent and situated art practitioner. She instigated and curated conversations and follow-on actions that drew in users excluded from the decision-making regarding the future of the market concerned.

In contrast to OS31's video-making session, which ran over the course of just one day, Helen's position as an artist-in-residence permitted a longer engagement with the users. This arguably permitted her to gain a greater degree of trust from her participants, as she was able to meet with them on a number of occasions and to initiate, sustain, develop and reflect on the conversations that she curated.

Referring back to Burns & Kahn's terms, her project operated with relational, social and experimental understandings of site. She utilised particular 'modes of representation' in order to stage and document provocations that allowed her to appreciate the more nuanced and invisible aspects and complex dynamics of site ownership (as this is understood beyond a basic legal, property-based relationship). Moreover, she had time within the duration of the residency to plan how best to mobilise this input in a way that deliberately 'thickened' the understanding of the site. Not only did this challenge the top-down approach to the market – and disrupt the comfortable existing relationship between client and architect – it also supported the production of certain stakeholder mappings that could allow the communities of everyday users of this facility to understand more about their own contributions to (and positions within) a complex but invisible web of socio-cultural space.

Creative surveys and archaeological methods

Related to the methods involved in the OS31 and Helen Stratford case studies are those that have been developed over two decades by muf architecture/art. muf have a wide palette of approaches to support thick understanding of site through creative surveys.

muf's well-known project for Southwark Street (undertaken for the London Borough of Southwark in 1997) was developed as a pilot scheme that intended to provide a shared ground between public and private interests. Among a range of methods, muf orchestrated conversations with local residents, retailers, developers and businesses. While the understanding gained from these methods has informed – and been synthesised with – physical understanding, snippets of these conversations have also been preserved directly by being cast into the pavement and wider pedestrianised areas. As a material echo of this gesture, these pavements also incorporate local materials, using shingle from the nearby River Thames as aggregate.

This approach has a certain resonance with the artist Mark Dion's deployment of archaeological methods. His project *Tate Thames Dig* (1999)[5] linked spatially and programmatically with the development of Tate Modern near muf's Southwark Street site. While Dion's notion of archaeology is deliberately mis-applied to give value to the flotsam and jetsam washed up in Thames mud, another of muf's projects – the St Albans Hypocaust Pavilion project (2004)[6] – deals directly and materially with ancient archaeological remains, revealing and framing the remains of a Roman building to casual users of a park and deliberate visitors alike. In this case, the building literally becomes a viewing device through which the archaeological remains can be protected and experienced insitu.

Dion sits within a broad trajectory of land artists working from the 1960s onwards, whose sensitivities and curiosity are legible in Loyn & Co's attitude to site and materials, introduced in their Stormy Castle case study. These architects retain control over the ways of looking while broadening their lens, revealing a quasi-archaeological attitude towards place that responds to geological, and human and physical geographical, clues.

Institutional Critique

While the land artists deliberately turned their backs on the gallery system to make work outdoors, other artists were expanding art's response to the gallery system itself, leading to the emergence of alternative art spaces and practices that are known as 'institutional critique'. The broader motivations of Helen Stratford's work operate in this way, opening up the invisible operation of institutions to view in such a way that their processes can be questioned, challenged, supplemented or expanded.

Similarly, Lynch Architects set out to understand site as much as a social construction as a physical location, and the critical curiosity towards site described in their case study places their knowing cultural production within a long lineage of spatial practice that is as much time-based and institutionally critical as it is material.

Extending this institutional critique into the spaces offered by new media technologies, architectural practices are increasingly addressing an expansion of the site of architecture, and architectural knowledge, into the virtual world. Many of the methodologies mentioned above inform or accompany this move, which also mobilises new relations of cultural production and new forms of power associated with the development of new media.

The work of Architecture 00 explores how the site of architectural production – and the operation of the cultural architect – can move online. In projects such as 'The Place Station: Reclaiming Underused Assets for Community Use',[7] or muf's 'Open Spaces that are not Parks' (2004),[8] these practices operate as cultural enablers or intermediaries, using their architectural awareness to put potential users in touch with potential sites of action, developing a tradition that can be linked back to Cedric Price.

Appropriating other methods for cultural research in practice

As Gillian Horn's case study demonstrates, this kind of cultural understanding can also be explored directly as a research project, such that its architectural implications are not immediately harnessed by architectural, artistic or enabling projects (as in action research), but shared as an outcome in their own right, made available for others to learn from and respond to.

Horn's work undertakes to demystify those 'socially constructed' aspects of site that circulate as public taste. Again closely linked to pioneering work by land and conceptual artists such as Gordon Matta-Clark or Hans Haacke (and to sociologists such as Pierre Bourdieu) the 'value' of property is little understood by the public, so can frequently be manipulated by vested interests. In contrast to prevailing architectural writing on value and judgement – and we can trace this back as far as that Vitruvian cliché prioritising firmness, commodity and delight – Horn's evidence-based research underwrites a careful rebuttal of many systems that are taken to be so self-evident that the profession (and the public) take them for granted.

More broadly and metaphorically, all the practices mentioned here can be understood to adopt expanded ways of looking and seeing, informed directly or indirectly by cultural studies. They can provide both encouragement and rationale for the cultural architect, and they can increase awareness of cultural and other value systems embedded in different, as well as familiar, methodologies. Cultural methods, particularly those developed by art practice, can offer potential tools for adoption or adaption by architects.

---

1   A useful background work for anyone interested in the development of Cultural Studies is R. Williams (1958), *Culture and Society* (London: Chatto and Windus), in which Williams explored and developed a new understanding of the development of western 'culture'.

2   A. Kahn, 'On Inhabiting "Thickness"' in S. Ewing, J.M. McGowan, C. Speed & C.V. Bernie eds. (2011), *Architecture and Field/Work* (London: Routledge), p. 56.

3   C.J. Burns & A. Kahn, (eds.) (2005), *Site Matters: Design Concepts, Histories, and Strategies* (London: Routledge).

4   R. Krauss (1985), *The Originality of the Avant-Garde and Other Modernist Myths* (Cambridge, MA: MIT Press).

5   For more details see I. Blazwick (2001), 'Mark Dion's "Tate Thames Dig"' *Oxford Art Journal* **24**(2), pp. 105–12; Tate (n.d.) *Mark Dion: Tate Thames Dig learning resource* (Tate: www.tate.org.uk/learn/online-resources/mark-dion-tate-thames-dig).

6   For more details see M. Fraser (2013), *Design Research in Architecture: An Overview* (Farnham: Ashgate), pp. 124–125.

7   www.theplacestation.org.uk

8   muf (2004), Open Spaces that are Not Parks (muf: issuu.com/mufarchitectureartllp/docs/openspaces).

Chapter 15

POP-UP BUILDINGS IN THE CITY

TONY BROOMHEAD, OS31

CONTRIBUTOR PROFILE: TONY BROOMHEAD

Tony Broomhead is an architect and founder of OS31, working with communities and public bodies across the UK to develop interactive and accessible architecture. He also teaches at the University of Sheffield School of Architecture, specialising in film as a means of representation – work that also informs OS31's approach.

In recent years there has been an increased emphasis on the involvement of communities and user groups in the architectural process. Through a series of projects working with communities, youth groups and local authorities we have established a methodology that uses film to develop briefs and inform design work. This 'live' research is critical to our practice and is at the core of everything we do. We see this research as an ongoing process and our approach will continue to evolve with each new project. Methods for public engagement or evaluation are rarely included in the teaching in schools of architecture. Practices like muf and AOC combine techniques from the conceptual art world with the analytical skills of the architect to develop consultation events and games. These new methods go a long way towards making the engagement process a useful tool for architects; our research took their work as a starting point as we formalised our own approach.

Practice profile: OS31

OS31 is a newly founded (2014) collaborative micro-practice interested in responsive, adaptable and interactive architecture. The main driver behind OS31's research is their desire to encourage debate and empower users. They believe that by doing this a more resilient architectural agenda can be developed, resulting in spaces that are focused on human interaction. The practice's architectural research practice provides them with a mechanism for testing out ideas; they use film and other recording media as research tools at key points within projects to inform designs.

CONTEXT

In 2009 we were invited by Lancaster City Council to do a one-day workshop with a group of 14-year-olds from four diverse schools across the city as a part of the Square Routes project. Our task was to work with the children to explore new ideas for Market Square, an important and popular civic space that was due for redevelopment. We had no fixed brief, and there were no expected outcomes other than the display of any work produced at the City Library. For us this was the perfect opportunity to test and develop film-based techniques.

APPROACH

Philosophy

We wanted to let the youth group lead the process, by allowing them to use a medium they understood. By doing so the project could then be used to instigate debate and let the children have a genuine impact on the future of their city.

A mind-map
by Lancaster
schoolchildren

Methods

Our method had three distinct stages: raw footage, rough cut and final cut.
These roughly map to the data collection, data analysis, and final analysis/
conclusion and dissemination research stages.

Raw footage

The first – and most important – step was handing over power to the teenagers
involved with the project; this was our time to listen and learn. The 20 children
were split into two equal groups – one group had digital video cameras, and the
other had sound recording equipment. The groups were given research
questions to think about while recording, for example 'What is good about
Market Square? How do people use it?' These open questions were just a
starting point; we wanted their footage to evolve naturally. The children then
spent two hours documenting Market Square through interviews, soundscapes
and other methods. We were on hand to help, but not to interfere.

Rough cut

After lunch we all came together to review the raw footage, projecting the videos
so everyone could get involved. It was a fun and relaxed session in which people
got to chat about the films, and some values started to emerge. In this case it
became about the square being seen as an event space, the importance of
lighting, and how the square should link to other spaces. The group then started
to select videos that embodied these values. With our help, they roughly edited
together a five-minute film that expressed their agenda.

Final cut

The footage was taken back to our studio in order to formulate a visual brief.
This was partly a packaging exercise in order to collate the visions that had been
revealed through the rough cut, but also acted as a generator for design ideas.

We combined the footage with drawings and precedent images to show the aspirations of the youth group, and to give it more impact.

INSIGHTS AND IMPACT

The Lancaster project represents the coming together of several ideas that had evolved over a three- or four-year period. It wasn't formally called research at the time, it was more about finding different ways of engaging with user groups. From each workshop or test we learned something, and the processes were refined. For example, while teenagers are happy to film everything, they will drift away from the point they want to make; older people may have more focus, but are reluctant in front of the camera. Therefore we learned to adjust the time frame of the workshops depending on the age group.

The youth group invited stakeholders from within the City Council, the landscape designers and the local community to a screening of the final film. We had pulled together many of the disparate views of the various bodies involved into one coherent package, and opened up the dialogue between the different stakeholders. As a result of the film the then-current proposal for Market Square was put on hold and the design approach reassessed. We were invited to work with both the Council and the landscape architects to develop a strategy for a number of civic spaces, to lead on to a wider consultation process.

This small project shows that a bottom-up approach can have an impact when issues and ideas are expressed in an accessible medium. The aim wasn't to show that a group of 14-year-olds know best, but to allow them to have a voice and to encourage debate. We are very proud of the project and its impact, with some of the ideas from the film forming part of the regeneration scheme.

LESSONS

Our agenda was to formulate an approach to public engagement, and to test different approaches. We have always seen a value in this, as we feel it keeps practice fresh and avoids us making lazy assumptions about what people want.

As architects we have a broad skillset, but in order to remain current we feel it is important to constantly explore new ways to apply these skills. Since the Lancaster project we have continued to use film as a primary means of engagement, but our methods will continue to change as we gain experience working with various groups, and as technology becomes more sophisticated. It is vital that we give time to this type of research, and we build it into our fee proposals. We justify this to our clients by showing that investing at the beginning of a project can make the design process easier further down the line and lead to better design.

Chapter 16

MARKET MEDITATIONS

HELEN STRATFORD, HELEN STRATFORD ARCHITECTS

CONTRIBUTOR PROFILE: HELEN STRATFORD
Helen Stratford is an architect whose work is located between architecture and visual/live art; since 2003 she has practised professionally in both fields, with architectural practice forming a critical frame of reference for her research.[1] She previously worked at practices Mole Architects and 5th Studio.

Her work and research has been presented in national and international forums, including: ICA, Tate Modern and RIBA (London); P74 and Škuc Gallery (Ljubljana); Akademie Schloss Solitude (Stuttgart); The Living Art Museum (Reykjavik); Barnard College (New York) and École des Beaux-Arts (Paris). Recent work includes projects for Fermynwoods Contemporary Art; Cambridge Junction; Norwich Arts Centre; Smiths Row, Bury St Edmunds; Forest Fringe and METAL.

M arket Meditations sought to explore a performative approach to post-occupancy – RIBA Plan of Work Stage 7 – as a form of critical architectural practice. The project explored how an architectural research-led project that foregrounds performativity and architecture through active/social terms sas a 'site of group co-ordination in space over time',[2] might employ performance-based methodologies and practices to research and produce space. Working towards developing a new body of work that explores a playfully critical approach to urbanism through visual, performance and live-art practices, it sought to understand how such practice differs from conventional architectural practice, asking 'What kind of space does it produce?'

Practice profile: Helen Stratford
Helen's work in practice is interdisciplinary and aims to engage with and make visible alternative ways of constructing knowledge about place. Her research relates to the way architecture produces certain ways of behaving, yet requires movement and interaction with the body to be understood. In this interrelationship, buildings and public space are perhaps better understood as 'performative conditions' – 'acting on us and activated by us'.[3] Performative in this case means how public spaces are produced and performed through everyday activities, routines, legislations and policies. Her architecture-led research explores daily routines and performances that exist inbetween planned spaces, which contribute to their production. Through site-specific interventions, live-art events, video works, speculative writing and discursive platforms she explores the politics of everyday life, searching for modalities that expand the conventions of architecture.

CONTEXT

Funded by Zavod Celeia (Slovenia), the British and Arts Council International Artists Development Fund, and conducted as research towards a practice-led PhD in Architecture at Sheffield University (funded by an RIBA LKE Ozolins PhD Studentship), Market Meditations formed part of a residency at the Center for Contemporary Arts, Celje, Slovenia in 2013–14. In recent years, Celje, Slovenia's third largest city (with a population of 40,000) has been undergoing a regeneration programme led by the city authorities.

Located in the centre of the city, the market building was one of the first buildings in this programme. The result of a public competition in 2006, it was completed in 2010 by Ark Arhitektura Krušec. Designed to replace an unstable and largely self-made structure, the building has been shortlisted for multiple awards, including the Mies van der Rohe award and the Public Space award. However, the market traders have another story to tell. The traders

During the performative workshops in the market, students from Celje high school tried out unexpected actions, including 'meditating'

make amendments to the space around them quite expertly, yet for many the building is non-functional: they feel limited in their capacity to make the space their own.

APPROACH

Philosophy

Market Meditations sits within a wider body of research that develops practice-based tools and actions that then feed back into architectural research. Informed by feminist theories of 'situated knowledge' and the production of subjectivities and space in relation to human agents and non-human actors, these tools and actions research how public spaces are performed and how certain power relations and hierarchies are supported.

Methods

Following street-survey style conversations with the market traders to discuss their concerns, students from the Gimnazija high school, were invited to join curator Maja Hodosček and I in a performative exploration of the market building. The research took place over two workshops, at the school and the market. After discussing typical uses for the market – what people did and when, how people acted, which spaces they used and for what actions – the students were asked to develop new actions/instructions for ways the building might be performed differently, or how it might be used once the traders leave. The project was conceived both as a proposal and provocation.

After a slow start, the students tried out activities in the market, including 'Hide and Seek', 'Tennis', 'Massage' and 'Meditation'. They hid under, stood, sat and leant on the white terrazzo tables, interacting with the traders who joined in the playful actions, including arranging flowers around one prone student. Finally, a poster of instructions written by the students for future users was put on display by taping it to the wall of a concrete water fountain in the centre of the market. It was about an hour before it was removed...

INSIGHTS AND IMPACT

When the new market building first opened, the story of the discomfort of a number of traders with its functionality was made public in the local and national press.[4] However, their continuing dissatisfaction and inability to make long-term changes, compounded by the design protection afforded to the building by the Slovenian architectural code of conduct, was not common knowledge.[5]

A public exhibition in autumn 2014 provided a means of disseminating the workshop actions as well as offering points of discussion around the use and design of the building. Ultimately, the students' actions offer an intermediary space of transition. Their actions are not constrained by the laws that restrict the traders' ability to make changes, and in addition – even if momentarily – they also step outside the architects' vision, reflected in the way the space is currently used, supported by CCTV cameras and signs which forbid playful activities such as skateboarding. In this context, the students' actions challenge this vision and open up new possibilities for the space, offering both critical insight and performative potential for future users.

LESSONS

One key aspect of my research practice, overlooked prior to Market Meditations, was the provocative nature that not only makes existing practices and performances visible, but actively encourages people to perform the spaces they inhabit every day differently, and to think about them differently. These provocations were something that Market Meditations explored in detail, looking at how critical tactics and strategies – which place oppositional (and often conflicting) visions of cities, public spaces and buildings together – might form useful research tools for further development.

Personally, Market Meditations marked a departure in my practice, as I invited others to devise site-specific actions rather than setting them up myself. This proved extremely effective in terms of participant engagement from students and traders alike, but also in attracting the attention of the newly appointed Market Director, activating a point of discussion between those who determine the use of the space and those who work within it.

1   For architectural historian/theorist/designer Jane Rendell this interdisciplinary position is a defining characteristic of Critical Spatial Practice. This is a term that Rendell formally introduced in her 2006 book *Art and Architecture: A Place Between* (London: I.B. Tauris), but is also defined in her 1999 journal article 'A Place Between' *Public Art Journal* **1**(2).

2   Shannon Jackson (2011), *Social Works: Performing Art, Supporting Publics* (London: Routledge).

3   Doina Petrescu, presentation at Performative Architectures discussion event, organised by urban (col)laboratory at the Showroom, London, October 2011. Also see: European Platform for Alternative Practice and Research on the City (PEPRAV) (2007), *Urban/Act Practices, Groups, Networks, Workspaces, Organisations, Tools, Methods, Projects, Data & Texts: A Handbook for Alternative Practice* (Paris: AAA/PEPRAV), p. 319.

4   One article in *JANA*, a Slovenian family magazine, refers to the new building as a 'mausoleum'. It reports that the municipality opened the new market, saying it represents the heart of the city, but goes on to comment that 'If this market is the heart of the city then it needs a cardiologist because, in the middle of the cold, wind and lack of traders/customers, this heart isn't functioning'. Tina Nika Snoj (2009), Zgrešena celjska tržnica [Misguided Celje marketplace] (JANA/Zarja: www.revijazarja.si/2009/12/zgresena-celjska-trznica/).

5   Article 20 of the Slovenian Code for architects, landscape architects and spatial planners stipulates that consent must be gained from the architect for amendments to public buildings.

Chapter 17

BUILDING WITH LANDSCAPE

CHRIS LOYN, LOYN & CO ARCHITECTS

CONTRIBUTOR PROFILE: CHRIS LOYN
Chris Loyn is Principal Architect of Loyn & Co Architects, based
in South Wales, and a visiting tutor at the Welsh School of
Architecture (WSA) and at the Centre for Alternative Technology
(CAT) in Machynlleth. He is also a painter and a member of the Royal
Watercolour Society of Wales.

M uch of Wales is open countryside with rolling hills and mountains, a context that brings particular difficulties when considering development proposals and seeking an appropriate architectural response. Historically, rural buildings have been primarily concerned with shelter and have been nestled in hollows of protection, away from the prevailing wind. How to use today's technology and materials to create a contemporary architecture for the rural environment of Wales has been a key area of research of the practice for many years.

The practice is equally interested in the 'performance' of projects as it is in the joy we aim for them to bring. Natural light, views through and beyond, and creating space and place that allows instinctive interaction with its specific occupiers are all critical. Rural architecture can be both functional and aspirational – something the practice is striving to promote in the context of Wales.

Practice profile: Loyn & Co Architects
Founded in 1987, Loyn & Co is a small practice of six. The practice works primarily on residential and commercial projects.

The practice's research is grounded in their projects, through a reflective design research process of development, testing and ongoing evolution. Previous and current schemes are regularly reviewed in the studio environment and lessons learned in a process of refinement, constant learning and development.

CONTEXT

The project considered here is Stormy Castle, a purpose-designed, low-energy, low-maintenance, sustainable, Code 5, site-specific lifetime family home. The site lies in a remote and exceedingly sensitive rural setting on the Gower coast, Wales, on the edge of National Trust land, occupying an elevated, prominent hillside position. It lies within a designated Area of Outstanding Natural Beauty.

In many ways, this was as much a landscape scheme as a piece of architecture, with the building needing to sit *in* the site rather than *on* the site. Considerable time was spent working with the landscape architects, researching the history and topography of the site through painting and sketches, and investigating the changing field patterns and the species of plants and grasses. This is a home designed to settle and mature within its surrounding landscape, and to suggest a new approach to sustainable, site-specific, low-energy passive design in rural housing.

APPROACH

Philosophy

Our approach to the project adheres to our philosophy of tectonic design – of understanding materials before designing the solution; of letting the materials express themselves honestly and beautifully. This is key to the development of our working drawings and details at concept design stage: we knew what we were building with, how and why we were building with it.

Methods

As the concept evolved we undertook research to determine the most appropriate form of construction. We prepared a matrix to analyse the preferred selection of materials, taking particular account of issues of locality and access, lifespan/longevity, sustainability, maintenance and durability, and cost and appearance. We also visited other projects and suppliers to assess first-hand the products under consideration.

Principal materials selected for the project were insitu concrete, using up to 50 per cent of locally sourced ground granulated blast-furnace slag (GGBS), a logical material for an earth-sheltered construction, with elements of Corten and strategically positioned expanses of glass. This combination proved cost-effective – and gives low maintenance and longevity to the building – while providing a raw, honest aesthetic appropriate to the site and the harsh environment. Concrete is widely used in the local agricultural buildings, as is rusted metal, which also tones with the rich brown-orange of the surrounding bracken and wider landscape.

Spatially, much time was spent physically and digitally sketching and modelling to refine the concept in close liaison with the client and, latterly, organisations such as the Design Commission for Wales (DCfW). The aim was to integrate site analysis with the developing form, ensuring that sufficient levels of ever-changing light would penetrate deep into the building. Sunlight warms and reflects the polished concrete floors that flow up and through a series of interlinking, unique, yet adaptable spaces. Layout, material selection and the framing of views come together to form a home explored via journeys: from the agricultural to the refined; from dark to light; from new to old.

This large yet low-impact dwelling can only be seen in its entirety from an aerial view, with the majority of its fragmented form concealed and cut into the hill, indistinguishable from the landscape. Elements of Corten continue inside specific areas, while careful consideration was given to spaces which were cut into the hill, designed from the inside out. The accommodation was planned to take account of room function and sun path, thus creating surprising light-filled volumes to move through and experience. Internal finishes were applied and restricted to non-load-bearing insertions or areas carrying voids for services; similarly ground-bearing stairs became ramps between two levels, whereas others were floating open risers. Refinement of the design resulted in a consistent tectonic approach and a cohesive language across the design, bringing the outside in and the inside out.

INSIGHTS AND IMPACT

The project has surpassed all targets set at the time of the client's original brief. These include achieving Code 5 for Sustainable Homes, an EPC rating A (following a 100/100 score) and an actual CO_2 building emissions rate (BER) of *minus* 0.46 kg/m^2 against a target emissions rate (TER) of 22.55 kg/m^2. The building uses a combination of a highly insulated fabric, including green roofs and technological systems – such as ground-source heat pump and mechanical ventilation and heat recovery (MVHR) – to achieve its credentials.

Stormy Castle was completed in December 2013. In 2014 the building won the Manser Medal, an RIBA Regional award, the National Eisteddfod Gold Medal for architecture, a Concrete Society award and a CIBSE Sustainable award (2013). The finished product is a testament to the strong relationship between client, architect, design team and contractor. Since completing the scheme, we have had several enquiries and are embarking on other significant rural developments which will embark from the research undertaken on Stormy Castle.

The client for Stormy Castle was awarded the Royal Society of Architects in Wales 2014 Client of the Year. The careful layers of systematic research that underpin the scheme were made possible through the client's commitment to creating a contemporary home for the Welsh landscape.

LESSONS

Construction in remote areas – where access is often extremely difficult – using technologies with which many contractors are unfamiliar, and with high expectations for attention to detail and quality of finish, is difficult. Couple this with unpredictable weather, and you find that achieving the desired standards can prove challenging.

Despite conducting interviews at tender stage, and explaining in considerable detail ideas and expectations, these were often misunderstood or misinterpreted by those actually undertaking the work on site.

Ensuring that the workforce appreciated that a self-finished product requires care and protection was at times very challenging. This is a stage in the process of realising a piece of architecture that we have been improving on in our more recent projects; communication with the makers is vital.

Stormy Castle

Chapter 18

SCULPTURE AND ARCHITECTURE IN THE MODERN CITY

PATRICK LYNCH, LYNCH ARCHITECTS

CONTRIBUTOR PROFILE: PATRICK LYNCH
After studying architecture at Liverpool University (1987–93) Patrick Lynch gained a MPhil degree in the History and Philosophy of Architecture at Cambridge University (1996). He subsequently gained a PhD at the Cass School of Architecture (2014) – while also teaching and working as an architect in London – developing his research into the relationships between sculpture, architecture, festivals and cities.

As both a practising architect and a scholar I seek understanding,
knowledge and a philosophical foundation for my imaginative work. The
scale of projects that we are now undertaking at Victoria Street in central
London entails the creation of some major public spaces, and the role of art and
landscape design in these spaces cannot be underestimated. Understanding
their role, and the role of architecture in this dialogue, is my aim.

CONTEXT

Our client for the Victoria Street project is Land Securities, whose estate
encompasses almost the entire street, and whose ambition is to create 'a new
city quarter'. The project includes the creation of a number of public spaces and
gardens, as well as four new buildings designed by us, and half a dozen large
projects by other architects. An ad hoc master plan has evolved over the past
eight years of our involvement with the project, and our buildings address
relationships between key civic institutions – such as Westminster Cathedral,
City Hall and Victoria Station – emphasising their roles as part of a renewed
high street.

The historic importance of our site compels us to create architecture of
decorum, the precise nature of which is the subject of my research.

View of the new Victoria Library from Victoria Station

APPROACH

Philosophy

While at Cambridge, I studied the influence of Baroque festivals on the design of urban spaces, particularly the role of the Zwinger in Dresden. The role of nature, myth, history and tradition is clear in Renaissance culture, and my subsequent research at the Cass has shown that these topics remain relevant to contemporary praxis, and continue to influence modern architecture and sculpture. I continue to investigate the potency and meaning of these themes in hermeneutic terms, both in deepening my philosophical understanding of the relationship between art, theatricality and cities, and in practical terms as buildings that incorporate art as ornament. My work as an architect emphasises the vital role that art plays in the communicative aspect of civic space.

My approach is twofold. There is interpretation (hermeneutics), which builds on the writings of Plato and Aristotle concerning terms such as poetics and mimesis, practical wisdom and ethics, and seeks continuity of these themes in modern culture. Then there is direct engagement with buildings via participation in events (phenomenology). Both are of course influenced by twentieth-century 'practical philosophy', and in particular I have emphasised the vital contribution of Hans-Georg Gadamer (*Truth and Method*,[1] *The Relevance of the Beautiful*,[2] *Reason in the Age of Science*,[3] etc.). I have also been influenced by the work of my teachers Peter Carl, Dalibor Vesely and Joseph Rykwert.

Methods

My work is a critique of the pseudo-scientific methods that architects attempt to appropriate from the social and natural sciences, and of art historical criticism that disengages aesthetics from praxis.

I have worked in a practical and imaginative way with artist collaborators, in creative dialogue about the limits and possibilities of public art commissions. Based on historical examples – knowledge of which I gained via research and travel, collating it in drawings and written interpretations – we have discussed the traditional roles of nature, ornament, wealth and civic pride in artist–architect collaborations, as well as the importance of recent terms such as economic, ecology and technology in the renewal of civic collaboration.

Our designs have been tested in public forums (including public meetings and consultations with individuals and local residents' groups), in exhibitions and furthermore in dialogue with Westminster Public Art Panel and specialists within the Westminster planning department. The research has involved a certain number of interviews with architects and artists, including Rafael Moneo and the family of Eduardo Chillida.

INSIGHTS AND IMPACT

Through the research I discovered that not only was art of the past made for practical and poetic reasons, but also that this tradition continued even in late twentieth-century buildings which are otherwise considered aniconic, such as St Peter's Church at Klippan by Sigurd Lewerentz. As well as exhibiting aspects of my work in Venice, we also disseminated parts in an exhibition catalogue, *Civic Architecture: The Facades, Courts and Passages of Westminster*,[4] at the Building Centre. The work will be published in two further books this year.

Our ability to articulate what we think is at stake in the urban situations that we encounter has been of enormous benefit in speeding up the planning process for our client; the creation of a decent civic realm on Victoria Street has not only secured excellent tenants for our clients, but has also enabled the planning department to articulate its aims as policy.

By identifying the traditional role of architecture as a setting for sculpture – not as sculpture per se – and in emphasising the role that nature plays in ornament, we have been able to unite contemporary thinking about sustainability with urban design, both theoretically and practically. This has led to new commissions on problematic sites that exhibit what I can now see is typical twentieth-century thinking about the city in terms of zoning, technology and so on.

LESSONS

We are now able to articulate better not only the problems that we are encountering as architects at the moment, but also to see that these problems are cultural ones resulting from a particular theoretical position, i.e. technology-based modern architecture and urban design. We are able then – being equipped also with knowledge of historical practice – to approach other urban sites and projects as typical urban problems. We will continue to further our knowledge and deepen our experience in the field.

1   H-G. Gadamer (1975), *Truth and Method* (New York: Seabury Press).

2   H-G. Gadamer, trans. by N. Walker (1986), *The Relevance of the Beautiful and Other Essays* (Cambridge, UK: Cambridge University Press).

3   H-G. Gadamer, trans. by F.G. Lawrence (c.1981), *Reason in the Age of Science* (Cambridge, MA; London: MIT).

4   P. Lynch & D. Grandorge (2014), *Civic Architecture: The Facades, Courts and Passages of Westminster* (London: Lynch Architects).

Chapter 19

THE TASTE FOR NEO-VERNACULAR HOUSING

GILLIAN HORN, PENOYRE & PRASAD

CONTRIBUTOR PROFILE: GILLIAN HORN

Gillian Horn has been in architectural practice for 20 years, the last ten as a partner at Penoyre & Prasad. She has been involved in a number of research-led design projects, including the DfES Building Schools for the Future and the multidisciplinary Space for Personalised Learning. She is a chair of CABE's London Design Review panel and a member of Urban Design London's Housing and Public Realm Design Surgery panel.

My interest in understanding why such consistently criticised, poor-quality, neo-vernacular housing is being produced in the UK has grown over my years in practice. I am now undertaking a research doctorate, funded by the White Rose College of Arts and Humanities, that investigates the formation and influence of taste on the behaviour of housebuilders and homebuyers, and the extent to which this limits the design quality of new housing. My findings will be fed back and tested in practice.

The exercise of taste is one of the ways in which we define who we are and, as such, is an important dimension in our sense of satisfaction and well-being, but little is known about the actual parameters of consumers' tastes in housing. There is widespread criticism of the design quality of volume housebuilder developments. The shortage of housing supply, the primacy of location and he short-term interests of housebuilders (maximising profit) tend to be cited as causes of this, but rarely are the tastes and preferences of housebuyers considered.

Organisation profile: Penoyre & Prasad

Penoyre & Prasad is a London-based large–medium architectural practice of over 30 staff, founded in 1988. The practice works across a number of sectors – including residential, health, education, workplaces and master planning – and specialises in sustainable design and retrofit.

The practice believes in the value of research-through-design and design-through-research. It actively engages in and promotes research projects, which recently include:

- A building performance evaluation in-use strategy, funded by Technology Strategy Board (TSB, now Innovate UK) of Crawley Library with Oxford Brookes University's Institute for Sustainable Development's Low Carbon Building Group.
- TSB-funded Design for Future Climate project developing strategies to adapt UK buildings to climate change; using the current QEII hospital project as a 'live' case study, and working with Oxford Brooks University and the project design team.
- TSB-funded multidisciplinary Retrofit for the Future project to reduce carbon emissions in existing housing stock.

Penoyre & Prasad have collaborated with Oxford Brookes University for the last ten years, undertaking regular post-occupancy evaluations of their projects and measuring the actual environmental performance of their buildings with the aim of bringing a rigour to their intentions and process, and to ensure that their design solutions continue to be pragmatic and efficient.

CONTEXT

Nearly half of all new homes in the UK are built by the top ten volume housebuilders, who were noted in the *Calcutt Review of Housebuilding Delivery* as 'not [being] in business to serve the public interest, except incidentally. Their primary concern is to deliver profits for their investors, now and in the future.'[1] An Office of Fair Trading study of the market also highlighted that with the importance of price and location dominating house purchasing choices, in a market where new supply outstrips new demand by a ratio of two to one, sales and increasing prices are not a necessary indication of buying choice.[2]

Research has shown that after location, external appearance – and in particular a period style – is cited as an important priority to the vast majority of homowners, with more respondents rating the importance of these aspects of their homes than the size, décor and quality of the rooms. Newly built homes in the UK are also the smallest in Europe. Why do we value looking-at over being-in?

APPROACH

Philosophy

'Taste classifies, and it classifies the classifier' asserts the French Marxist sociologist Pierre Bourdieu, observing that 'Tastes (i.e. manifested preferences) are the practical affirmation of an inevitable difference.'[3] While *Distinction*, his seminal work, provides a research-based theoretical grounding on class and taste to work from, references in my research are necessarily broad, to capture the multitude of themes that influence our taste judgements. Goffman and Giddens bring perspective on modern identity,[4] Davis and Boym on nostalgia,[5] Dorling and Piketty provide an economic context[6] and Kahneman adds evidence-based insights into how we make intuitive judgements and decisions.[7]

Methods

I am investigating public perceptions and housebuilder assumptions of consumer taste from industry, public and policy perspectives by researching past, present and possible future aesthetic perceptions of the home. This includes analytical drawings of familiar typologies, looking at the impact of the familiar ingredients in neo-vernacular housing by way of structured interviews with prospective buyers, developers, architects and planners.

Stripping back Poundbury

INSIGHTS AND IMPACT

This research project offers the space and framework for considered and systematic investigation and exploration of consumer taste in architecture that any one individual project in the practice couldn't otherwise support, in terms of either time or finance.

Tastes in housing are formed from many threads of influence. The powerful grip of money and ideas of home are tightly interlocked within strands of identity, security and familiarity interweaving with lines of continuity, connection and association, fashioning a potent and complex tapestry of conditioning.

Aesthetic judgements in housing cannot be separated either from seemingly objective assessment criteria, such as 'value for money' or 'a good location' or from intangible, subjective influences such as 'homeliness' and 'nostalgia'. We seek a *look* of home because it is significant to us to *feel* at home. And with the housebuilding and housebuying market set within, not outside, this self-reflexive embroidery, the discriminations of taste become so pervasive and appropriated that they assume effective cultural invisibility. Unpicking this tapestry of taste and challenging the inevitability of the pattern that has been woven by the various threads of influence is a step towards exploiting the real potential of design in housing, which is currently being marginalised by unthinking prejudices of taste.

LESSONS

I would encourage every practice to engage in structured research. As a profession it is essential, since research takes us forward. A particular benefit of structured research is the means for more effective dissemination it brings, and with that the potential for wider impact and change based on the findings.

Casting a wider net of enquiry beyond the specifics of a project's demands and requirements brings fresh insights and approaches into practice, shared as new findings, references and avenues for exploration. People are at the heart of an architectural practice, and interest is at the heart of our approach. Penoyre & Prasad encourages research sabbaticals for the fresh spirit they bring individuals and in turn the collective.

I think research is a refreshing and upbeat way of connecting professionally and of bringing a wider context of purpose to our work. At a time when the status and value of the profession is being persistently eroded, research offers some means of resistance and pushback, in territories that we can choose to define.

---

1   J. Callcutt (2007), *The Callcutt Review of Housebuilding Delivery* (Wetherby: Communities and Local Government Publications; webarchive.nationalarchives.gov.uk).

2   Office of Fair Trading (2010), *Home Buying and Selling – a Market Study*, OFT1186 (Office of Fair Trading: webarchive.nationalarchives.gov.uk).

3   P. Bourdieu (1984), *Distinction: A Social Critique of the Judgement of Taste* (London: Routledge & Kegan Paul).

4   For example see Philip Manning (1992), *Erving Goffman and Modern Sociology* (Stanford University Press) and Anthony Giddens (1991) *The Consequences of Modernity* (Polity Press).

5   See F. Davis (1977), 'Nostalgia, identity, and the current nostalgia wave', in *Journal of Popular Culture*, **11**, pp 414–425.; Davis, F. (1979), *Yearning for yesterday: A sociology of nostalgia* (New York: Free Press); Svetlana Boym (2001), *The Future of Nostalgia*, (New York: Basic Books).

6   See for example D. Dorling (2014), *Inequality and the 1%* (London Verso Books) and Thomas Piketty (2014), *Capital in the Twenty-First Century* (Insert 'D. Kahnemann (2011), Thinking, Fast and Slow (London: Penguin, 2012).).

7   D. Kahnemann (2011), Thinking, *Fast and Slow* (London: Penguin, 2012).

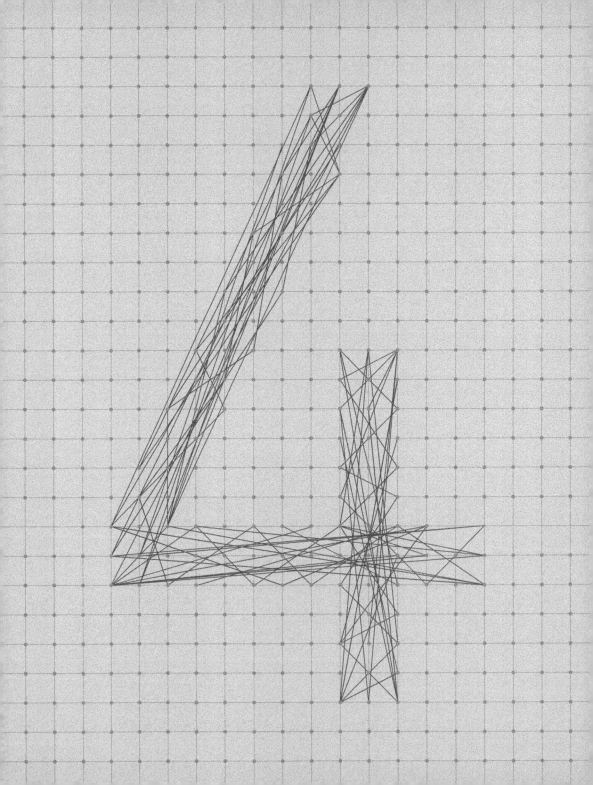

Part 4
Commercial Research Practice

Chapter 20

DEMYSTIFYING COMMERCIAL RESEARCH METHODS

ANNE DYE, ROYAL INSTITUTE OF BRITISH ARCHITECTS

CONTRIBUTOR PROFILE: ANNE DYE
Anne Dye is Head of Technical Research at the RIBA, responsible for
delivering the research agenda in alliance with the RIBA Research
and Innovation Group. This includes the development, support and
promotion of a range of strategic built-environment research projects
within the RIBA, in partnership with other organisations and within the
wider research community, as well as providing advocacy for research
to key stakeholders.

CONTEXT

'People often reject creative ideas even when espousing creativity as a desired goal.'[1] Why should this be, and what are the implications for architects – particularly architects in commercial practice?

Research published by Cornell University's ILR (Industrial and Labor Relations) School suggests that when people wish to reduce uncertainty (and so risk), an unconscious bias against creativity is activated.[2] And, as a recent series of roundtable discussions at the RIBA highlighted,[3] risk is a significant concern for commercial clients. This is one of the reasons why, for architects in commercial practice, skills related to addressing certainty and risk (such as those below) are advantageous.

Skillset of commercial architects[4]

- **Appraisal of financial viability** – translation of construction knowledge into the language of business.
- **Ability to maximise investment potential** – the planning, design and implementation of a development, redevelopment or regeneration project with multiple uses of a single prime use, the success of which is predicated on financial viability.
- **Efficient business practice** – leadership and planning to reduce risk to the client.
- **Conversant with patterns of consumption** – understanding and application of knowledge about retail, marketing, real estate and related fields.
- **Regulatory and planning compliance** – maintaining standards while maximising value.

These skills go hand in hand with a number of types of research that also support commercial architectural practice. What is particularly important in research in commercial practice is that it leads to actionable insights. This means that exploratory research is likely to play a lesser role in a commercial practice's projects (though it might form part of the a practice's own research) and that other methodologies – especially those that are well known and command the client's confidence, including those from other fields such as statistics, the physical sciences, or historical and legal disciplines (as Gordon Gibb uses in his work – will dominate.

But research can also help to lessen the impact of the risk-averse nature of very commercial clients on practice, helping clients to understand and value the creative skills of architects – or by acting to change the environment in which architects practice, for example by influencing the policy around procurement, which Walter Menteth has been working towards. This chapter explores some of these methods, and their relevance to commercial practice.

USING RESEARCH TO INFORM PROJECTS

Where there is a need to carry out research to support a commercial project it is likely that there will be a very specific use intended for the results and insights from the project which will lead to focused research questions. The research questions will help you focus the review and minimise the time and resources needed to collect relevant and useful evidence.

You and your clients will also want to make sure that you can have a high degree of confidence in the results of the research. This doesn't necessarily mean favouring quantitative data over qualitative, but it does require care and attention to detail throughout the research process.

Before undertaking research for a project it is also important to have a good grasp of the current knowledge on the subject. Staff may have collected literature related to the subject, and this can be a good starting point for a review. You need to decide whether a traditional literature review or a systematic review will meet your project's needs better – see box, below. A full systematic review may not be called for, or affordable, but you may want to incorporate some of the aspects of it into your literature review, such as using rigorous inclusion and exclusion criteria for evidence, or using more than one reviewer to reduce bias, this can make a traditional literature review more authoritative. Alternatively you might consider a 'rapid appraisal'[5] which has some characteristics of a systematic review but is less time-consuming to produce.

Doing (or reviewing) systematic reviews and rapid appraisals might be particularly useful for healthcare buildings where evidence-based design is well embedded. But all types of project and client can benefit from insights derived from previous research and projects.

Existing buildings are often useful when talking with a client as examples of what can and cannot be achieved in a new project. While this might be done informally through a guided visit to a practice's building, it is worth remembering that case study analysis is also a formal research strategy, which can use qualitative or quantitative methods. Case study research is especially suited to complex situations and multidisciplinary phenomena – such as buildings and their interactions with their users and context – with multiple sources of evidence. One source of evidence that may be useful in case studies is post-occupancy evaluation (POE), and its big sister building performance evaluation (BPE).[7]

Traditional vs. systematic review

	'Traditional' literature review	Systematic review
Methodology	Not defined, can be more or less systematic, flexible	Structured, rigorous, transparent, replicable
Analysis	Reflective, explorative, narrative	Synthesis, meta-analysis (a statistical method)
Advantages	Can consider research that might be excluded by strict criteria of systematic review, helps develop critical skills	Authoritative and can be influential (e.g. in a policy context); important information source for evidence-based policy and practice
Disadvantages	Subjective, risk of biased analysis, no requirement for quality assessment of material	Time consuming; relies on access to databases; must assess all relevant literature; may be difficult to apply to cross-disciplinary evidence
Can be used to identify research gaps?	Yes	Yes
Number of researchers	Can be undertaken by one person alone	Bias can be reduced by using more than one researcher
Main features	Research question – can be broad Iterative, exploratory methodology Subjective	Might be preceded by a traditional, scoping review Research question – often focused Methodology planned before commencement; progress documented Inclusion and exclusion criteria Uses quality criteria
Output	Discursive narrative	Brief answers to research questions, often tabulated

Summarised from Jesson et al.

By formalising your case study processes your insights will be more authoritative and more likely to persuade a sceptical client. You may also want to consider multiple case study analysis, where you can explore concepts and ideas in greater detail, either to inform a particular project or the practice's work in general. Robert Yin's book *Case Study Research: Design and Methods* is possibly the most useful resource for those starting to do formal case study research.[8]

Research is not just something external that informs briefing and design, but can be an integral part of these processes. Often, a piece of research will have an experiment (testing the impact of one or more specific variables on outcome of interest)[9] at their heart – a powerful methodology, as it has the potential to establish causal links.

Modelling – experiment's powerful ally (with an Achilles heel)

It is not always possible to do physical experiments for either practical or ethical reasons. For example, you probably wouldn't want to set fire to a completed building to assess spread of fire and effectiveness of evacuation.

Modelling or simulation, can help overcome these issues. A model can be either physical, for example using salt baths to model heat flow and natural ventilation[10], or virtual, which is becoming progressively more sophisticated as computing power continues to increase. Software can model physical properties – such as daylight, energy consumption or thermal response – or behaviour, such as crowd movement through stadia. Alternatively it can provide a different way for people to interact with a proposed design, such as through the use of virtual reality headsets, and provide evaluation feedback. These can help architects to make informed design decisions, evaluating the pros and cons of different options.

But simulation does not always predict the actual behaviour of the completed building. Why? Are the maths or physics wrong? Are the assumptions about things like human behaviour too generalised? It turns out to be a mixture of reasons but in particular the difference between as-designed and as-built – even where issues are 'small', such as mortar bridging a cavity wall or half a brick in a ventilation duct[11] – can have big impacts on performance and it is rare that the building is actually used as the client predicted. This can lead to large discrepancies between modelled and actual performance – the so-called performance gap.

This type of research can, for example, help a building meet sustainability aspirations under challenging circumstances such as in the heat of Abu Dhabi. For the Al Bahr Towers, modelling (physical and virtual) helped refine the design and performance of a contemporary and adaptive interpretation of a traditional *mashrabiya* shading screen which reduces solar gain by up to 50 per cent.[12]

Another experiment might be about how to improve the pedestrian flow through, and experience of, a railway station – as for the refurbishment of Kings Cross station in London. Arup, working with the architects Stanton Williams, used the pedestrian modelling methods Legion,[13] STEPS[14] and Pedroute when evaluating pedestrian flow through the station.[15] In particular the Legion model allowed the team to look at the impact of types of pedestrian (commuters, those with reduced mobility, those with luggage), train timetables and issues such as those whose tickets are rejected by the ticket barrier and need to seek assistance.[16] Arup disseminates its research outcomes and profits from sales of its journal. Others have dedicated research journals[17] which help to promote their practice through research.

USING RESEARCH TO INFORM PRACTICE, BUILD REPUTATION AND A PRACTICE USP

While much research in commercial practice is likely to be related to specific projects, other more speculative research projects can yield significant and long-lived advantages to a practice – advantages that far outweigh the resource implications. These projects might be exploratory; at the outset you may not be sure what type of insights you might find or even whether they will be useful or not, perhaps using methods such as Grounded Theory (see box, below). Alternatively they might answer specific questions that could be useful in informing the practice's work, perhaps by doing statistical analysis of records from a database of the practice's POEs.

Exploratory research; developing theory

An explanatory study might use quantitative methods (such as statistics or graphical analysis) or you might want to analyse information from your practice qualitatively, either to see whether an existing research question is worth pursuing (testing a theory) or to develop an entirely new theoretical understanding of your practice, project or clients.

One way to do this is to use a method such as Grounded Theory, where a theory is developed by looking for connections in raw data (for example from your own site notes, design team meeting minutes, focus group audio recordings, or even quantitative data such as that from POE) in a systematic way,[18] similar to the way research is analysed in a literature review. The process of analysis is called coding, and can be done by hand, or by using software packages such as the free AQUAD 7,[19] CAT (Coding Analysis Toolkit)[20] or CATMA (Computer Aided Textual Markup & Analysis).[21] A quick web search will yield the most up-to-date free tools, or you might consider a commercial package such as NVivo[22] – especially if you intend to do many studies.

By using codified procedures such as Grounded Theory analysis to evaluate qualitative data you reduce the risk of bias, and are more likely to develop truthful (and useful) theory.

A good example of an exploratory study would be the collaborative study of the impact of flat-panel displays on trading room design[23] undertaken by Pringle Brandon.[24] The study both addressed prior client criticisms of the practice's approach and directly led to work that made the practice 'world-wide market leaders overnight'.[25] It has also had a lasting impact on both the practice (it is still an important part of the practice's marketing, reflecting the impact it has had on the practice's profile and reputation among clients)[26] and the profession, having been included in the *Metric Handbook*.[27]

Statistical methods
Statistical studies can be very powerfully persuasive in influencing clients and policymakers, but must be applied with care. Correlation does not always imply causation and, while studies with small samples open up new avenues of enquiry, be careful if using them to give 'an indication' of what the answer might be.

Using generalised research methods can lead practices on to develop their own research tools or to market specialised research services to their clients.

Some commercial research services offered by architecture practices

Tool/Service (practice)	What it is	Research methodology (more information)
WorkWare, WorkWareLEARN and WorkWareCONNECT (Alexi Marmot Associates)	A suite of five methods looking at how buildings are used	POE – statistical and case study, quantitative and qualitative (aleximarmot. com/workware)
BUS (building use studies) methodology (Arup)	Domestic and non-domestic POE, used on the PROBE studies in the 1990s	POE – statistical and case study, quantitative and qualitative (www. busmethodology.org)
Rapiere (Architype, BDSP, Greenspace Live and Sweett Group)	BIM-compatible carbon, energy and cost-modelling tool	Modelling/Simulation (rapiere.net)
Conservation reports (Baxter & Associates LLP)	PPS5 statements, Heritage Impact Assessments, conservation management plans, views analyses, Conservation Area studies	Historical – architectural history graphical (alanbaxter.co.uk)

SELLING RESEARCH SERVICES

Developing research in a practice that is not linked to particular projects, and so is likely not to have restrictions on how widely it can be disseminated, allows a practice to really develop its research skills and related tools. These can then be commercialised, bringing further financial benefits and cementing the practice's position as a market leader.

Having a research speciality also allows a practice to offer one-off research services, which all add to the practice's knowledge base and standing. Projects of this type include:

• Bringing together complex issues into guidance in *Building for Life*[28]
• Mapping and applying existing housing standards[29, 30]

These examples of research – across projects, practice and services – are just a sample of the myriad that can thrive in commercial practice. For those yet to develop research in their practice they can offer inspiration about how to get started, while for those looking to expand their research, this material flags a few additional avenues worth exploring.

1 J. Mueller, M. Shimul & J. Goncalo (2010) *The Bias Against Creativity: Why People Design But Reject Creative Ideas* (Cornell University's ILR School: digitalcommons.ilr.cornell.edu/cgi/viewcontent.cgi?article=1457&context=articles) quoted in F. Samuel, N. Awan, C. Butterworth, S. Handler & J. Lintonbon (2014), *Cultural Value of Architecture: A Critical Review with Specific Reference to Homes & Neighbourhoods* (University of Sheffield: www.culturalvalueofarchitecture.org).

2 *Ibid*

3 For example see M. Thompson (2014), *Listen and Learn* (RIBA Journal: www.ribaj.com/intelligence/listen-and-learn) and M. Thompson (2015), *Office Moves for the Better* (RIBA Journal: www.ribaj.com/intelligence/offices-are-back-on-the-architects-agenda).

4 F. Samuel, N. Awan, C. Butterworth, S. Handler & J. Lintonbon (2014) *Architect Types and their Skillsets* (University of Sheffield: www.culturalvalueofarchitecture.org).

5 GSR (2008), *Government Social Research Civil Services Rapid Evidence Assessment Toolkit* (GRS: www.civilservice.gov.uk/networks/gsr/resources-and-guidance).

6 J.K. Jesson, L. Matheson & F.M. Lacey (2011), *Doing Your Literature Review – Traditional and Systematic Techniques (London: Sage)*.

7 See Chapter 1 for more discussion of post-occupancy evaluation.

8 R. Yin (2014), *Case Study Research: Design and Methods* 5th ed. (Sage: Thousand Oaks).

9 L. Groat & D. Wang (2013), *Architectural Research Methods* 2nd ed. (New Jersey: Wiley), Chapter 9, p. 316.

10 For an interesting discussion about how an architect and a scientist have worked together see A. Short & A. Woods, BP Institute (2010), *Naked Engineering – Natural Ventilation* (Cambridge University: www.thenakedscientists.com/HTML/content/interviews/interview/1460).

11 Max Fordham (1999) (conversation with author).

12 AHR (n.d.) *Al Bahr Towers* (AHR:www.ahr-global.com/Al-Bahr-Towers).

13 www.legion.com/legion-software

14 www.steps.mottmac.com

15 A. Jenkins & C. Rooney (2012), 'Planning for Pedestrians' *Arup Journal*, 2, pp. 23–25.

16 *Ibid*

17 Research journals published by practices include The Perkins + Will research journal available at perkinswill.com/research; Scott Brownrigg's *iA: Intelligent Architecture*, available at www.scottbrownrigg.com/about/design-research-unit/overview/

18 A. Strauss & J. Corbin (1998), *Basics of Qualitative Research* 2nd ed. (London: Sage), pp. 11–12.

19 Available from: www.aquad.de

20 Available from the QDAP (Qualitative Data Analysis Program) of the University of Massachusetts Amherst: cat.ucsur.pitt.edu

21 Available from www.catma.de

22   Available from www.qsrinternational.com/

23   Pringle Brandon (1996), *20/20 Vision: A Report on the Impact of Flat Panel Displays on Trading Room Design* (London: Pringle Brandon).

24   Now Pringle Brandon Perkins + Will, part of the global Perkins + Will group

25   arq (2003), 'Is the RIBA taking research seriously? At long last, it looks as if it is', *Architectural Research Quarterly*, **7**(2), pp. 104–106.

26   Pringle Brandon Perkins + Will (2014) *Portfolio Insurance* (London: Pringle Brandon Perkins + Will), issuu.com/pringlebrandonllp/docs/portfolio_insurance_2014.

      Perkins + Will (2012) *Pringle Brandon Joins Forces with Perkins + Will* (Perkins + Will), perkinswill.com/news/pringle-brandon-joins-forces-with-perkins-will.html.

27   D. Littlefield ed. (2012) *Metric Handbook: Planning and Design Data* (Abingdon: Architectural Press), pp. 12–18.

28   See the Mæ website, www.mae-llp.co.uk/projects/by-name/building-for-life-guide.html

29   Richards Partington Architects (2010), *Mapping Existing Housing Standards* (CABE), webarchive.nationalarchives.gov.uk/20110118095356/www.cabe.org.uk/files/mapping-existing-housing-standards.pdf.

30   CABE and Richards Partington Architects (2010) *Applying Housing Standards: London Case Studies* (CABE), webarchive.nationalarchives.gov.uk/20110118095356/www.cabe.org.uk/files/applying-housing-standards.pdf.

Chapter 21

WORKING AS AN EXPERT WITNESS

GORDON GIBB, GIBB ARCHITECTS LTD

CONTRIBUTOR PROFILE: GORDON GIBB
Gordon Gibb set up Gibb Architects immediately after his Part 3,
before studying Law and accepting a part-time appointment to teach
Professional Studies. As part of the ARB/RIBA Working Group he
rewrote the Part 3 criteria, before being elected to the ARB as Vice
Chair. He acts as an adjudicator and mediator, and is a consultant for
the RIAS.

Traditionally when things go wrong in construction – even if the architect is only partly to blame – their professional indemnity insurance can be involved, simply because suing an insured party is more likely to achieve some level of success. In the past the architect often stood alone. Increasingly, however, a team approach is taken by parties seeking to reclaim sums on larger projects with non-traditional appointments, and the obligations and liabilities of design team members are seen as overlapping. In liability claims, the view of apportionment between design and inspection activities has also changed over time, as has the number of parties that may make a claim.

All of these changes, and evolving risks for architects, need to be addressed. Research into the field is needed in order to benefit education processes as well as the profession's exponents and reputation.

Organisation profile: Gibb Architects Ltd

Gibb Architects Ltd is a micro-practice based in Glasgow. The practice has designed and administered housing, commercial and historic buildings for nearly 30 years. Gordon Gibb has also acted as an expert witness in construction disputes, writing reports and appearing in court. The practice is now involved in most aspects of dispute resolution. Gordon is also involved in the development of professional education for architects.

The practice undertakes research to support its expert witness work, and believes its reputation is built on the quality of that work. Research is required for most of its expert witness commissions to analyse physical evidence and to inform opinions. An architect expert witness provides guidance to a court on what constitutes normal practice, underpinned by an understanding of how buildings are put together, how a construction team operates and what an architect should know; this is a constantly changing field of knowledge.

CONTEXT

Few authoritative texts on the management of risk in the industry discuss the dynamics of claims and liabilities in the light of evolving contract provisions and procurement methods. My work as an expert witness is underpinned by forensic analysis of correspondence, consultants' drawings, specifications, photographs and reports on building failure. When I analyse these documents for court I must give consideration to the legal and contractual obligations, and deliver findings; this forms the basis of my court testimony.

I have built up a body of cases (for which I have produced over 150 reports) and knowledge of trends in dispute resolution – underpinned by a clear

Extension to India of Inchinnan, Renfrewshire, Scotland by Gordon Gibb

understanding of contractual matrices and professional obligations. It is on this evidence, along with the authoritative texts, legal outcomes and the advice of others in my field, that the research has been built.

APPROACH

Philosophy

An expert witness will search for the truth, based on evidence analysed in the light of their professional knowledge. This underpins their opinions which are checked for their impartiality by asking 'What would I say if I was on the other side?'

I wish to support my profession, to help it deliver for its clients the services they need, providing architecture under new procurement challenges. I also wish to help the student body avoid the pitfalls that await the unwary. I have found that to scrutinise the evidence more means you need to opine less – a lesson I wish I could disseminate more widely among my peers.

Methods

Through tabulation of my cases from the last three decades – by dispute, field of claim against the architect, other parties involved and amount claimed – I was able to systematically review the contract provisions alleged to have been breached, and why. I also considered whether the method of dispute resolution adopted had any impact on the outcome of the case.

INSIGHTS AND IMPACT

A number of key findings emerge from the research:

- The received wisdom in the construction industry – that under Design and Build the number of claims against architects would fall – is incorrect. While the number of 'inspection failure' cases has dropped, the number relating to design or design coordination has risen.
- Net contribution clauses have made it harder to make a claim against the architect in respect of a loss which was principally the fault of the contractor. Because of this there has been a change in the nature of claims, moving from 'failure to inspect' or 'over-certification' to 'failure to coordinate the input of others' – a factor of design for which the architect is normally fully responsible.
- There has been a change in the liability matrix in many construction projects. Procurers of architecture have changed appointments to strengthen the architect's obligation, while reducing client risk. These changes include: the use of clauses that make the architect liable to both the contractor and the client at the same time; whistleblowing clauses, to make the architect liable for specification changes imposed by the contractor under design and build contracts and the use of the designation 'lead designer' in design and build, to make the architect liable for the integration of all aspects of design into the whole.
- Architects are often caught out by believing, incorrectly, that an obligation they hold sits with another party, under non-traditional procurement arrangements, after novation – architects may still be obliged to inspect. Clauses are also written so that the contractor may claim against the architect that they employ, even in respect of the contractor's own deficiency in meeting the employer's requirements. The employer may also claim against the architect for a design failure or a failure to warn through a collateral warranty.

In all of this there are a number of conflicts of interest for the architect, the principal one being that it will be hard to maintain a good working relationship with a contractor-client while complying with an obligation to tell the employer that the contractor is in default. Risk is increased because many architects don't understand the obligations they signed up to. A key message – based on the research – is to scrutinise contract documents, because it is within the building contract, and not just their own appointment, that the full extent of the architect's obligation lies.

However the findings are not all negative:

- In design and build, although the contractor is still the first port of call in any claim for design or building failure, design teams and contractor-designers are brought into the action – often in multi-party mediations. Each party claimed against brings its own team to the debate, and this spreading of liability is now complicating and slowing the resolution of claims against contractors. For future employers this may increase their perceived risk, and make design and build less attractive.
- It is being found, in retrospect, that in non-traditional procurements the lack of an independent design-led project officer has allowed poor practice in specification or workmanship resulting in building failures. The proliferation of such cases may result in revision of contract provisions to reduce specification-busting, and may encourage the development of a more dominant architect role post-contract.

I believe that other architects could benefit from the knowledge I've gained through my work and research – as my practice has done – so I disseminate my findings through teaching and consultancy work for the RIAS, my expert witness appointments and blogging on LinkedIn and at www.gibbarchitects.co.uk/blog.

LESSONS

This research project has been illuminating for the practice, and has produced tangible and relevant results and insights. My work has stressed the need to understand risk and to guard against being caught out by the wording of a contract or by a difficult client. Architects would do well to take advice before, rather than after, the calamitous event and may find that the appropriate option is to walk away from the commission at the outset.

I would recommend that others follow a similar path: forming a hypothesis, based on something that may be perceived as a change or development in the practice of architecture, in an area where the practitioner has an interest. A good place to start looking for a research topic is, in my view, in the practice's own files.

Chapter 22

MARKETING ARCHITECTS

PAUL IDDON, AGENCY SPRING

CONTRIBUTOR PROFILE: PAUL IDDON

Paul Iddon is UK Managing Director and co-founder of Agency Spring.
He originally trained as an architect and practised for 19 years, co-
founding two practices during the 1990s, including OMI Architects,
Manchester. Since 2010 Paul has been developing brand and
engagement strategies with architects and manufacturers. Paul is a
council member of the Manchester Society of Architects and lectures
regularly at universities across the UK.

The majority of architects in the Western world are experiencing unprecedented falls in fees, personal income and relevance. The re-alignment of the built environment value chain to focus on profitable and timely delivery models has favoured the growth of intermediate management and has displaced the traditional role of the architect as the contract supervisor/project manager/client agent. Decline in trust by clients and moves to eliminate risk have resulted in the growth of the novation of architects as subcontractors. The growth in new entrants to the building design 'market' and increase in replacement services have further undermined the core offering of the profession.

The current paradigm is not delivering value for the profession in terms of status and remuneration, except for the top 10 per cent who dominate the field, commonly referred to as 'starchitects'. It is clear that a major re-alignment is taking place in the sector; the question that remains is what the future of the architect will be in the value chain.

Agency profile: Agency Spring
Agency Spring – an Anglo-Danish branding and communication agency – has 115 staff in four offices – Copenhagen, Aarhus, Manchester and Ho Chi Minh City. They work in both business-to-consumer (B2C) and business-to-business (B2B) categories, working across product and brand creation to digital and analogue communication strategy, and media. They work with blue chip international companies and with built environment companies such as Icopal, Grundfos, Danfoss, Cembrit and VELUX (DOVISTA).

The agency (with its associate companies) has been active in many areas of consumer research since 2010. More recently they have extended this expertise into specifier marketing research, including usage and attitude, qualitative and quantitative as well as online analytics. Much of their research is commissioned projects with clearly segmented user groups. However they also undertake their own projects – most recently with architects and other specifiers to develop life-stage and attitudinal segmentation models aimed at helping manufacturers understand the construction market in depth.

CONTEXT

My own particular experience and skillset led me to believe that an analysis would be feasible to research the possible options for the architectural profession using marketing, sales and business management techniques that do not currently form part of the architect's arsenal.

APPROACH

The starting point was to consider the architects as a 'brand' in the classic marketing definition and then apply models developed by industry leaders such as McKinsey & Company, Philip Kotler and David Aaker to develop a new positioning strategy that would form the basis for a 'brand relaunch'. The ongoing project is to engage with actors in the value chain, in addition to architects themselves, to uncover insights that would be the foundation of the repositioning process.

Philosophy

Our starting point was the fundamental principle that architects are the most highly trained creative and strategic agents in the development of the built environment. By necessity an architect's training is long, difficult and broad-based, and the field has become increasingly specialised and occupied by niche suppliers. Our positive approach was to find new relevance for the architect through better understanding of their current place in the value chain, and develop evidence to support a new positioning.

Methods

We have conducted research using a variety of classical and digital techniques to gather quantitative and qualitative data that can then be used to form a picture of the current status of the architect. Interviews and focus groups are also being undertaken to identify the need states of clients, consultants, contractors and end users that could then be analysed to develop insights into possible positioning strategies.

According to our background research this approach has not been explored in any detail as it is generally considered 'difficult' by classical marketers due to considerable levels of bias and preconception in the profession and its surrounding institutions. We took the view that it is a valid exercise nonetheless, with significant benefits should it shift perceptions and build value in the architect brand. There is no technical or academic reason why this approach should not work. Initially we undertook desk research to establish precedent in this area, as well as reviewing literature, such as works by Eric Cesal, Rory Hyde and Adrian Dobson. The following key issues were identified:

• Brand relevance
• Brand identity and positioning
• Built environment category analysis
• Skill levels in basic business in practice
• Teaching of basic business, sales and marketing skills in schools of architecture
• Attitudes of other actors in the built environment value chain
• Architect attitudes to professional standards, skills and support
• Relevance of professional bodies in practice realities

We are currently in the process of setting up digital platforms to further segment the architectural profession according to attitudinal and life-stage preferences.

In addition, live projects undertaken with several practices, two in London and two in Manchester, have revealed that there is a desire to both understand and apply marketing techniques. This has been extended to include basic sales techniques to leverage better fees and also avoid no-win pitch scenarios.

INSIGHTS AND IMPACT

Our initial findings are that is it is extremely difficult to overcome inbuilt biases (as described by Kahneman)[1] in several segments of the audience. This is particularly prevalent in the older segments as well as the younger market entrants. The most engaged segments tend to be those in practice who are looking for some way to leverage better value in their business life. This is unsurprising given the economic pressures on most practice owners.

A lack of basic business skills is caused by a complex set of factors, including:

- Design-driven education
- Professional status still being highly relevant to older segments
- Lack of connection between design and clearly defined client benefits
- Frustration at requirement for more knowledge and skills to operate in an already devalued market
- Business skills being perceived as 'boring' or even viewed with hostility
- Lack of perceived relevance in the everyday life of the architect

A basic grounding in such knowledge is a prerequisite for at least some of the profession to be able to successfully apply tools and techniques that will enable better business results. It is clear that much more work needs to be done to understand personal and psychological drivers of many architects at different levels of education and life stage, and with different preferences.

LESSONS

There is much to be done, but there is a significant proportion of the profession that is looking for new ways to add value to their business and personal life.

A variety of tools and techniques can be developed to address the basic knowledge gaps in the professional, including undergraduate, postgraduate and in practice. These will need to be tailored to the experience of the particular audience. There is still a need to develop the language and approach to avoid alienating the audience in many cases.

Recent activity in USA shows that there is a hunger for a repositioning of the architect 'brand'; indeed the AIA is undertaking a mass-media campaign on exactly this subject to the value of approximately $1.5 million.

---

1   D. Kahneman, P. Slovic & A. Tversky (1982), *Judgment Under Uncertainty: Heuristics and Biases* 1st ed. (Cambridge, UK: Cambridge University Press).

D. Kahneman & A. Tversky (1996), 'On the Reality of Cognitive illusions', *Psychological Review* **103**(3), pp. 582–91.

2   *Ibid.*

Chapter 23

PROCUREMENT

CONTRIBUTOR PROFILE: WALTER MENTETH
Walter Menteth is Director of Walter Menteth Architects and a Senior Lecturer at the Portsmouth School of Architecture. He is also a Director of Project Compass CIC (community interest company), an RIBA National Councillor, Chair of the Trustees of the North Southwark Environment Trust, a member of the Cabinet Office SME (small- and medium-sized enterprises) Panel 2011-15, and was Chair of the RIBA Procurement Reform Group 2011–13.

H ow clients acquire professional services and construction works – and how an architect works within the procurement process – affects outcomes, quality, efficiencies, scoping, terms of employment and contract forms. The aim of this research into contemporary procurement was therefore to ascertain why the processes for the acquisition of services, supplies and works (both above and below the legal threshold values) set up under European treaties – intended to offer a fair, proportionate and open market – was creating increasing market skews and preventing UK design talent from gaining access to public work.

Practice profile: Walter Menteth Architects

Walter Menteth Architects is a micro-practice based in London, established in the 1980s. The practice works primarily on domestic, cultural, refurbishment, care, community and leisure projects.

The practice views research as an important part of all their projects, believing that it informs strategic and detailed outputs, while allowing them to optimise responses through a process of enquiry extending through to completion. Their research on public procurement supply chains and permissible contract forms grew out of their work on housing, and their experience that these elements had become incapable of responding to needs and opportunity.

CONTEXT

When the financial crash occurred in 2008 the similarities between some of the crash's causes and what was observable in the inherently dysfunctional construction procurement process fell into even sharper relief. After winning various housing awards and spending – as the practice estimated – a debilitating £250,000 applying for (and largely failing to attain) further public housing contracts by tortuous OJEU (Official Journal of the European Union) procedures, I decided to undertake a critique of current procurement practice. This decision was driven both by receiving circumstantial evidence on the subject from architect colleagues, and by learning that there was no other architectural research occurring in the field.

Rather than writing more pre-qualification questionnaires (PQQs), in late 2009 I started researching procurement in depth, gaining support from RIBA Housing and Small Practice Group colleagues. The research was sustained by patronage (including funding from an RIBA Research Trust Award in 2012[1]), along with emotional and titular support from a considerable number of colleagues without whom it would not have been possible.

My research fortuitously commenced shortly before the European Commission announced its intention to review existing procurement legislation. The subsequent publication of a green paper[2] opened up greater opportunities for the UK construction industry to have an impact on the reform process. I wrote our first formal report on the subject, *EU Green Paper – On the Modernisation of EU Public Procurement Policy – Towards a More Efficient European Procurement Market*,[3] in March 2011.

APPROACH

Philosophy

The work has been underpinned by a hypothesis that greater access and hence creative engagement by society in general, and the architectural community in particular, to public projects can deliver better social, environmental and economic value and opportunity for all. Like many architectural projects this research has developed into a far wider and more immersive engagement than initially anticipated.

Methods

The research has developed in an iterative style, organically, taking unexpected directions based on information acquired and unearthed. It was continuously informed and filtered by my own practice's experiences across a range of competitive processes in both the public and private sectors. In social science terms this would be action research, immersing oneself in the task at hand and working with others to solve it.

In July 2011 I was elected to the RIBA Council and, with the benefit of both the Council's and the then President Angela Brady's support, was appointed Chair of the RIBA Procurement Reform Group (PRG). The group allowed a wide range of construction sector interest groups and 42 individual participants, to draw together their experiences and inform findings, generating outputs that could contribute to the legislative reform process. I was also appointed to the Cabinet Office SME panel, enabling me to further gather cross-industry SME experiences.

The PRG developed a suite of four reports under the umbrella of *Building Ladders of Opportunity – How Reforming Construction Procurement Can Drive Growth in the UK Economy*.[4] These were developed over a short time period by establishing four independent voluntary working parties, each led by committed members who gathered content for the main report, with appendix case studies provided separately. All this with reference to the *RIBA Procurement Survey*[5] an independently commissioned legal overview.[6]

Amsterdam November 2014, attending Thefulcrum.eu presentation at Heat in the Delta conference

At each stage a period of consultation with a wide range of stakeholders was accompanied by the collection of other detailed evidence. The research involved data and statistical analyses, scrutiny of legal documents and opinions, commissioning of surveys, transcriptions of interviews, narrative constructions, referencing, checking, editing and so on.

Research, intelligence gathering and dissemination were coordinated with initiatives across the UK and the EU, for political the advancement of legislative reform. A number of EU, UK, Scottish and RIBA consultation papers have been drafted and edited en route.

Following receipt of RIBA Research Trust funding, a core group (comprising me, Russell Curtis and Owen O'Carroll, joined by Bridget Sawyers) established Project Compass CIC in order to further develop and refine digital tools for implementation. Under the auspices of Project Compass a website access portal[7] has been delivered, providing current UK construction-related OJEU tender notices, data, research and guidance. This digital infrastructure delivers a simple system that improves accessibility, for the purpose of supporting and sustaining implementation of the reform programme. Further research publications have also been issued.[8]

INSIGHTS AND IMPACT

My research finds clear evidence of a skewed UK market, reflecting a direct correlation between the growth of demand and inefficiencies in construction. It challenges many misconceptions in procurement about 'one size fits all', 'bigger is better', 'aggregation' and 'economies of scale' approaches, placing emphasis instead on proportionality, social value, intelligent commissioning and sustainability for achieving better-quality outputs efficiently – so that an improved architectural culture (capable of better engaging the public) can deliver economic advancement more effectively.

The project has contributed significantly to a collective drive towards reforming construction procurement legislation at EU and UK levels, with more than an estimated 85 per cent of recommendations put forward having been adopted. However, procurement culture is deeply embedded; the real litmus test will be whether new opportunities are effectively and efficiently adopted, along with the adoption of new e-procurement digital infrastructure.

LESSONS

The legal framework in which architects practice not only establishes what they do, but how, why, when, with whom and where they do it. Increasingly this is determined at European level and requires our fuller engagement – which is no bad thing – in a richer but more complex Continental debate. This not only provides important research and learning but also opportunities for reform, with the capacity to grow and advance UK architectural culture.

Although I am profoundly dyslexic and find the burden of paperwork daunting, my practice horizons have changed enormously for the better through this research. It has been an extraordinary pleasure meeting so many truly wonderful committed people en route, many who are now close friends, and I couldn't do anything but recommend taking up research as a strand in your own practice's work.

1   The RIBA Research Trust Awards are offered annually to support independent architectural research.

2   European Commission (2011), *Green Paper – On the Modernisation of EU Public Procurement Policy – Towards a More Efficient European Procurement Market* (Brussels: European Commission; eur-lex.europa.eu).

3   W. Menteth (2011), *EU Green Paper on the Modernisation of EU Public Procurement Policy – Towards a More Efficient European Procurement Market – Response Paper* (London: Walter Menteth Architects; eprints.port.ac.uk/13671/1/11-03-06_ EU_GreenPaperResponse_RevE.pdf).

4   RIBA (2012), *Building Ladders of Opportunity – How Reforming Construction Procurement Can Drive Growth in the UK Economy* (London: RIBA: www.architecture.com).

5   RIBA (2012), *Procurement Survey 2012* (London: RIBA: www.architecture.com)

6   Burges Salmon LLP (2012), *Comparative Procurement: Procurement Regulation and Practice in Germany, Sweden and the UK* (London: RIBA: www.architecture.com).

7   See www.projectcompass.co.uk/

8   For example W. Menteth (2015) *Summary of 'Public Construction Procurement Trends 2009–2014'* (RIBA: www.architecture.com/Files/RIBAProfessionalServices/Education/ Funding/2015/SummaryofFinalReport.pdf)

Conclusion

We wanted to create a book that showed the diverse nature of architectural research practice across the UK as an inspiration to others. It has been a pleasure in doing so to tease out the often unsung, but deeply impressive, research skills of professionals working at the top of their game. It has been our aim to illustrate that if the work of innovative practitioners can be translated into the more formal interdisciplinary language of research, then architectural research practice will be alive and well.

In 2012 we undertook a survey of research in practice that revealed that 43 per cent of practitioners believed themselves to be doing at least some research.[1] The rest believed that research was a good thing both for business and for their own professional satisfaction, but were unsure how to begin. They generally associated research with energy and performance or with the more esoteric aspects of theory; they did not see the connection with the way in which reflective practitioners try to make better buildings that are appropriate to their users, clients and context. As Leon van Schaik has observed 'Architects have come to believe that to do "Research" they have to stop practising and adopt arcane rituals and pseudo-objective writing styles.'[2] One of the aims of this book has been to dispel this myth. To do research is to work through a problem systematically and reflectively and then, ideally, to disseminate the results of that research.

The structure of this book derives from another of our research projects funded by the Arts and Humanities Research Council, this time on the Cultural Value of Architects in Homes and Neighbourhoods. We wanted to develop an evidence base for the value of architects' skills in generating well-being; however, our first hurdle was to define what those skills were. We realised that architects often appear to be at odds with one another because they are each working in very different value systems. We defined these as cultural value, social value, commercial value and technical value. Obviously there are overlaps in these systems, but we suggest that most architects have a dominant sphere of operation and use particular methodologies that relate to investigations in that sphere.

Identifying the ideology behind your work is really the first stage in defining methodology, a word that many practitioners find alarming, but is really just about saying as clearly and self-critically as possible what it is you do and why. Architecture as a field suffers from the fact that both practitioners and academics often operate with an unspoken set of rules learned through years of largely vocational training, and exposure to 'Archispeak'. It is this that makes the field so opaque to others, and has contributed to its marginalisation from the creation of the built environment, policy, research, society and dinner party conversation.

We argue that it is the lack of research culture in practice that has led to the state of affairs we are now in, where we are largely unable to prove, in a language convincing to policymakers, funders and others that architects actually make a difference. The situation is not helped by our professional journals, whose focus is not generally on research. We need to work together as a field to generate an evidence base of our value to be used when bidding for work, when applying for research funding, when arguing for or against planning and when fighting for a better-quality built environment. In response to the Social Value Act 2013 we need to be able to evidence the added social value of our schemes. We need to be able to state loud and proud the importance of architects' unique problem-solving skillsets.

Time of course is the issue in all this – time and money – but we would argue that architects already spend so much time on competitions with pitiful odds of success that they would be better off spending at least some time working on research projects – often with far greater chances of success, less risk, huge intellectual reward and the opportunity to develop a distinct practice offer. One of our motivations in writing this book was to encourage practitioners to bid for the €800 billion of Horizon 2020 funding currently available through Europe to address what they call the grand societal challenges – well-being, energy and so on – clearly within our remit. Another source of funding is through Innovate UK, for whom the primary criterion for success is showing that the practice will derive a business benefit from that research – and there are many more examples. We also want practitioners to go for funding as it is good business practice to have multiple income streams, making them less vulnerable to the vagaries of the construction industry. Additionally, and more importantly, research funding enables practitioners to work on ethically motivated projects that are not subject to the pressures of private finance. In many cases the first step in securing funding is finding an experienced academic researcher in an appropriate field to work. We are fully aware that our often inward-looking universities are also part of the problem, and we are currently working to develop a community of academics able and willing to support practitioner research across Europe.

IDENTIFYING THE IDEOLOGY BEHIND YOUR WORK IS REALLY THE FIRST STAGE IN DEFINING METHODOLOGY

All the practitioners included in this book derived value from their research, many of them economic value, and some were even paid to do the research by their clients. Research is, for example, central to the work of URBED who recently won the £250,000 Wolfson Prize for activities in this area. Research is written into the new RIBA Plan of Work, and is part of an expanded menu of services offered, for example by Architype. If you look at the homepage of Foster + Partners they clearly state that they are a research practice, and the Building Futures report *The Future for Architects?* suggested that specialised consultancy is the way forward. Research also carries a zero VAT rating, and has the potential to impact positively on insurance premiums, CDM and the pre qualification process.

ONE OF THE PREREQUISITES FOR FUNDED RESEARCH IS DISSEMINATION

One of the prerequisites for funded research is dissemination, something that practitioners often find particularly hard for a variety of reasons, not least because they are worried about losing their intellectual property. Without dissemination – without being able to identify innovation in a particular area – practitioners spend a great deal of time reinventing the wheel. Alarmingly, in the course of writing *Architects and Research-Based Knowledge*, we discovered that architects were more likely to consult their peers or Google than they were to use rigorous research findings.[3] We are fully aware that it is extremely difficult for practitioners to keep abreast of research developments, quite apart from the kind of technical innovation that is sometimes published in the annexes to the industry journals. Research journals will shortly become open access, which will help the flow of information, and they are not as turgid and technical as they used to be; we do however need to do more to disseminate our findings.[4]

The creative industries are set to take over from the financial sector as the foremost generator of income for UK plc, but within this architecture is experiencing a decrease in its market share. Architects, particularly SME practitioners, need to take a strategic step back to look objectively at why this is happening. All the evidence suggests that the problem resides in a lack of research leadership across the profession, a lack of systematic testing and evaluation of projects, and deficiencies in the ways in which architects demonstrate and communicate the value of their work. Only through research can practitioners make consistent improvements both in their outputs and the way in which they are communicated. Only then can the profession be what it set out to be, the strategic leader of the construction team and a force for good in wider discussions of the built environment.

We finish with a quote from Bentre Frost, mayor for city planning for Copenhagen, often called the world's most liveable city; 'Without the many studies from the School of Architecture, we politicians would not have had the courage to carry out the many projects to increase the city's attractiveness.'[5]

1   Samuel, F., Dye, A., Coucill, L. et al, RIBA Home Improvements Report on Housing Research in Practice, 2013, www.architecture.com/research

2   Leon van Schaik et al. (2010), Procuring Innovative Architecture (London: Routledge), p.33.

3   Collins, E. (2014), *Architects and Research-based Knowledge: A Literature Review* (London: RIBA), available at www.architecture.com/research

4   Intellectual property concerns can largely be addressed by delaying publication until after the breakthrough in question has been implemented

5   Jan Gehl and Birgitte Svarre (2013), How to Study Public Life (London: Island Press), p. 157

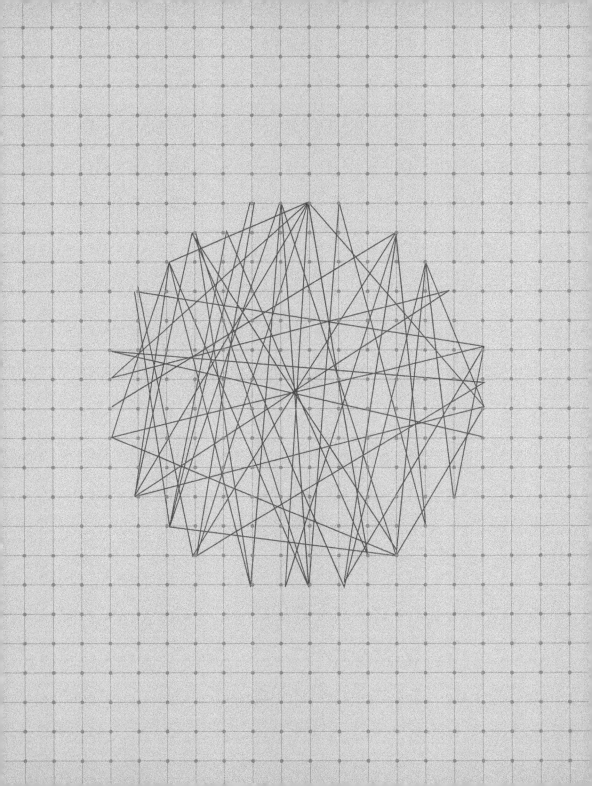

Bibliography

A

AHR (n.d.), *Al Bahr Towers* (AHR: www.ahr-global.com/Al Bahr-Towers).

arq (2003), 'Is the RIBA taking research seriously? At long last, it looks as if it is', *Architectural Research Quarterly*, **7**(2), pp. 104–6.

Awan, N., T. Schneider & J. Till (2011), *Spatial Agency* (Abingdon: Routledge).

B

Blazwick, I (2001), 'Mark Dion's "Tate Thames Dig"', *Oxford Art Journal* **24**(2), pp. 105–12.

Blundell Jones, P. D. Petrescu & J. Till, eds (2013), *Architecture and Participation* (Abingdon: Routledge).

Bourdieu, P. (1984), *Distinction: A Social Critique of the Judgement of Taste* (London: Routledge & Kegan Paul).

Boym, Svetlana. *The Future of Nostalgia.* New York: Basic Books, 2001.

BSRIA (n.d.), *Soft Landings* (BSRIA), www.bsria.co.uk/services/design/soft-landings.

Burges Salmon LLP (2012), *Comparative Procurement: Procurement Regulation and Practice in Germany, Sweden and the UK* (London: RIBA; www.architecture.com).

Burns, C.J. & A. Kahn, eds (2005), *Site Matters: Design Concepts, Histories, and Strategies* (London: Routledge).

Burnside, J. (2013), *Contemporary Design Secrets: the Art of Building a House in the Countryside* (Dublin: Booklink).

C

CABE and Richards Partington Architects (2010), *Applying Housing Standards: London Case Studies* (CABE), webarchive.nationalarchives.gov.uk/20110118095356/www.cabe.org.uk/files/applying-housing-standards.pdf.

Cabinet Office (2013), *Government Soft Landings* (Cabinet Office), www.bimtaskgroup.org/reports.

Callcutt, J. (2007), *The Callcutt Review of Housebuilding Delivery* (Wetherby: Communities and Local Government Publications), webarchive.nationalarchives.gov.uk.

Clemens, O. J. Fezer & S. Horlitz, eds (2008), 'Community Design: Involvement and Architecture in the US since 1963' *Anarchitektur.*

Collins, E. (2014), *Architects and Research-based Knowledge: A Literature Review* (London), RIBA: www.architecture.com/research.

D

Davis, Fred. *Yearning for Yesterday: Nostalgia, Art and the Society.* New York: The Free Press, 1979.

Department for Education and Skills, *Building Schools for the Future* (DfES) 2004, webarchive.nationalarchives.gov.uk/20130401151715/.

www.education.gov.uk/publications/
eOrderingDownload/DfES%200134%20
200MIG469.pdf).

Department for Communities and Local
Government (2013), Household Interim
Projections, 2011 to 2021, England (UK
Government, www.gov.uk).

Dorling, Danny. *All That Is Solid: How the
Great Housing Disaster Defines Our Times,
and What We Can Do About It*. London: Allen
Lane, 2014.

E

European Commission (2011), *Green
Paper – On the Modernization of EU Public
Procurement Policy – Towards a More
Efficient European Procurement Market*
(Brussels), European Commission; eur-lex.
europa.eu.

European Platform for Alternative Practice
and Research on the City (PEPRAV) (2007)
*Urban/Act practices, groups, networks,
workspaces, organisations, tools, methods,
projects, data & texts: a handbook for
alternative practice* (Paris: AAA/PEPRAV)

Ewing,S., J.M. McGowan, C. Speed & C.V.
Bernie (eds) (2011) *Architecture and Field/
Work* (London: Routledge)

F

Fraser, M. (2013) *Design Research in
Architecture: An Overview* (Farnham:
Ashgate)

G

Gadamer, H.G. (1975) *Truth and Method*
(New York: Seabury Press)

Gadamer, H.G, trans. by F.G. Lawrence
(c. 1981) *Reason in the Age of Science*
(Cambridge, MA; London: MIT)

Gadamer, H.G. trans. by N. Walker (1986),
*The Relevance of the Beautiful and Other
Essays* (Cambridge, UK: Cambridge
University Press)

Gething, B. & K. Puckett (2013), *Design
for Climate Change* (London: RIBA
Publications)

Giddens, Anthony. *Modernity and Self-
Identity: Self and Society in the Late Modern
Age* (Cambridge, Polity Press, 1991).

Goffman, Erving. *The Presentation of Self
in Everyday Life*. New Ed edition. London:
Penguin, 1990.

Green, S.D. (2011) *Making Sense of
Construction Improvement*, (Chichester:
Wiley)

Groat, L. & D. Wang (2013), *Architectural
Research Methods* 2nd ed. (New Jersey:
Wiley)

Government Social Research Service
(2008) *Government Social Research Civil
Services Rapid Evidence Assessment Toolkit*
(GSR), www.civilservice.gov.uk/networks/
gsr/resources-and-guidance.

H

Halligan, C. & J. Denison (2010), *The
Stephen George & Partners Guide to Building
Materials and the Environment* (Stephen
George & Partners: www.stephengeorge.
co.uk)

Hamilton, D. & D.H. Watkins (2009),
*Evidence-Based Design for Multiple Building
Types* (New York: Wiley)

Handler, S. & J. Lintonbon (2014)
Architect Types and their Skillsets
(University of Sheffield: http://www.
culturalvalueofarchitecture.org)

Harvey, D., (2012), *Rebel Cities: From the
Right to the City to the Urban Revolution*
(London: Verso Books)

Holder, A., (2014), *Initiating Architecture:
Agency, Knowledge and Values in Instigating
Spatial Change* (University of Sheffield: PhD
thesis)

Hopper, L. ed. *Landscape Architectural
Graphic Standards* (New York: Wiley)

Hulme, M., et al (2002), *Climate Change Scenarios for the United Kingdom: The UKCIP02 Scientific Report* (Norwich), Tyndall Centre for Climate Change Research, School of Environmental Sciences, University of East Anglia.

I

Infed.org (2007), *Action Research* (infed.org: infed.org/mobi/action-research

J

Jackson, S. (2011), *Social Works: Performing Art, Supporting Publics* (London: Routledge)

Jenkins, A. & C. Rooney (2012), 'Planning for Pedestrians' *Arup Journal*, **2**, pp. 23–5

Jesson, J.K., L. Matheson & F.M. Lacey (2011), *Doing Your Literature Review – Traditional and Systematic Techniques* (London: Sage)

K

Kahneman, Daniel. *Thinking, Fast and Slow*. London: Penguin, 2012.

Kahneman, D., P. Slovic & A. Tversky (1982), *Judgment Under Uncertainty: Heuristics and Biases* (Cambridge University Press)

Kahneman D., & A. Tversky (1996), 'On the Reality of Cognitive illusions', *Psychological Review* **103**(3), pp. 582–91

Klinenberg, E. (2012), 'Living Alone is the New Norm' *TIME*, **179**(10)

Krauss, R. (1985), *The Originality of the Avant-Garde and Other Modernist Myths* (Cambridge, MA: MIT Press)

L

Lefebvre, H. trans. by D. Nicholson-Smith (1991), *The Production of Space* (Oxford: Blackwell)

Lefebvre, H. trans by E. Kofman & E. Lebas (1996), *Writings on Cities* (Oxford: Blackwell)

Littlefield, D. ed. (2012), *Metric Handbook: Planning and Design Data* (Abingdon: Architectural Press), pp. 12–18

Live Projects (2014), One Great Workshop (University of Sheffield: www.liveprojects. org)

Lynch, P. & D. Grandorge (2014), *Civic Architecture: The Facades, Courts and Passages of Westminster* (London: Lynch Architects)

M

Mallory-Hill, S., W.F.E Preiser & C.G. Watson (2012), *Enhancing Building Performance* (New York: Routledge)

Matrix (1984), *Making Space: Women and the Man-Made Environment* (London: Pluto Press)

Matrix (1986), *A Job Designing Buildings: For Women Interested in Architecture and Buildings* (London: Matrix Feminist Design Co-operative)

McNiff, J. & Whitehead, J. (2002) *Action Research: Principles and Practice* (London: Routledge)

Menteth, W. (2011), *EU Green Paper on the Modernisation of EU Public Procurement Policy – Towards a More Efficient European Procurement Market – Response Paper* (London), Walter Menteth Architects; eprints.port.ac.uk/13671/1/11-03-06_EU_ GreenPaperResponse_RevE.pdf.

Menteth, W. (2015), *Summary of 'Public Construction Procurement Trends 2009– 2014'* (RIBA), www.architecture.com/Files/ RIBAProfessionalServices/Education/ Funding/2015/SummaryofFinalReport.pdf.

Morrell, P. (2015) *Collaboration for Change* (London: Edge: www.edgedebate.com/ wp-content/uploads/2015/05/150415_ collaborationforchange_book.pdf)

Mueller, J., M. Shimul & J. Goncalo (2010) *The Bias Against Creativity: Why People Design But Reject Creative Ideas* (Cornell University's ILR School), digitalcommons. ilr.cornell.edu/cgi/viewcontent. cgi?article=1457&context=articles).

muf (2004), *Open Spaces that are Not Parks* (muf), issuu.com/mufarchitectureartllp/ docs/openspaces).

N

Nowotny, H. (2015), The Cunning of Uncertainty (London: Polity).

O

O'Brien, R. 'Um exame da abordagem metodológica da pesquisa ação [An Overview of the Methodological Approach of Action Research]' in Roberto Richardson (2001), ed. *Teoria e Prática da Pesquisa Ação* [*Theory and Practice of Action Research*] (Universidade Federal da Paraíba: João Pessoa, Brazil); English version available at www.web.ca/~robrien/papers/arfinal. html

Office of Fair Trading (2010), *Home Buying and Selling – a Market Study*, OFT1186 (Office of Fair Trading), webarchive. nationalarchives.gov.uk.

One Great Workshop (2014–), Blog: *One Great Workshop* (University of Sheffield: onegreatworkshop.wordpress.com)

P

Pain, R. & Francis, P. (2003) 'Reflections on Participatory Research' *Area*, **35**, pp. 46–57

Perkins + Will (2012), *Pringle Brandon Joins Forces with Perkins + Will* (Perkins + Will), perkinswill.com/news/pringle-brandon-joins-forces-with-perkins-will.html.

Petrescu, D., (2007), *How to Make a Community as Well as the Space for It* (Republic), seminaire.samizdat.net/IMG/pdf/Doina_Petrescu_-2.pdf.

Piketty, T. (2014), *Capital in the Twenty-First Century* (Cambridge, MA: Harvard University Press)

Preiser, W. & Vischer, J. (2004), *Assessing Building Performance* (Routledge: Abingdon)

Pringle Brandon (1996), *20/20 Vision: A Report on the Impact of Flat Panel Displays on Trading Room Design* (London: Pringle Brandon)

Pringle Brandon Perkins + Will (2014) *Portfolio Insurance* (London: Pringle Brandon Perkins + Will; issuu.com/pringlebrandonllp/docs/portfolio_insurance_2014)

Public Works (2006) *If you can't find it, give us a ring* (ARTicle Press: www.publicworksgroup.net/publications/if-you-cant-find-itgive-us-a-ring)

Puthod, C., et al. (2000), *Creative Spaces: A Toolkit for Participatory Urban Design* (London: Architecture Foundation)

R

Reason, P. & H. Bradbury (2006), *Handbook of Action Research* (London: Sage)

Rendell, J. (1999), 'A Place Between' *Public Art Journal* **1**(2).

Rendell, J. (2006), *Art and Architecture: A Place Between* (London: I.B. Tauris)

RIBA (2009), *Charter and Byelaws* (London: RIBA: www.architecture.com)

RIBA (2012), *Building Ladders of Opportunity – How Reforming Construction Procurement Can Drive Growth in the UK Economy* (London: RIBA: www.architecture.com)

RIBA (2012), *Procurement Survey 2012* (London), RIBA: www.architecture.com.

Richards Partington Architects (2010), *Mapping Existing Housing Standards* (CABE), webarchive.nationalarchives.gov. uk/20110118095356/www.cabe.org.uk/files/mapping-existing-housing-standards.pdf.

Rudlin, D. & N. Falk (1999), *Sustainable Urban Neighbourhood: Building the 21st Century Home* (Oxford: Architectural Press)

S

Sadler, S. (1999), *The Situationist City* (Cambridge, MA: MIT press)

Samuel, F., et al (2013), RIBA Home Improvements: Housing Research in Practice (RIBA: www.architecture.com/research)

Samuel, F. et al (2014), *Architect Types and their Skillsets* (University of Sheffield), www.culturalvalueofarchitecture.org.

Schön, D. (1983), *The Reflective Practitioner: How Practitioners Think in Action.* (New York: Basic Books)

Short, A., & A. Woods, BP Institute (2010), *Naked Engineering – Natural Ventilation* (Cambridge University), www.thenakedscientists.com/HTML/content/interviews/interview/1460.

Strauss, A. & J. Corbin (1998), *Basics of Qualitative Research* 2nd ed. (London: Sage)

Studio Polpo (2014), OPERA #1 (Studio Polpo), www.studiopolpo.com.

Studio Polpo (2015), Blog: *OPERA #2 starts on Sunday 22nd March* (Studio Polpo), www.studiopolpo.com.

Studio Polpo (2015), Common Rooms (Studio Polpo), www.studiopolpo.com.

T

Tate (n.d.) *Mark Dion: Tate Thames Dig learning resource* (Tate), www.tate.org.uk/learn/online-resources/mark-dion-tate-thames-dig.

Thompson, M. (2014), *Listen and Learn* (RIBA Journal), www.ribaj.com/intelligence/listen-and-learn.

Thompson, M. (2015), *Office Moves for the Better* (RIBA Journal), www.ribaj.com/intelligence/offices-are-back-on-the-architects-agenda.

U

UK Climate Projections (2014), *Glossary > UKCIP02* (UK Climate Projections), ukclimateprojections.metoffice.gov.uk.

University of Sheffield (2013), *AHRC Home Improvements* (University of Sheffield), www.shef.ac.uk/architecture/research/homeresearch/home_research_projects/home_improvements.

University of Sheffield School of Architecture (n.d.) *Research Ethics and Integrity* (University of Sheffield), www.sheffield.ac.uk/architecture/research/ethics.

URBED, Tovatt Architects and Planners & Klas Tham (2009), *Design for Change Event – Brentford Workshop Outcomes* (URBED: urbed.coop/projects/brentford-lock-west)

V

Leon van Schaik (2010), *Procuring Innovative Architecture* (Oxford: Routledge)

W

Whyte, W.F.E. (1991), *Participatory Action Research* (London: Sage)

Williams, R. (1958), *Culture and Society* (London: Chatto and Windus)

Y

Yin, R. (2014), *Case Study Research: Design and Methods* 5th ed. (Thousand Oaks: Sage:)

YouGov (2012), *An Archi-what?* (YouGov), yougov.co.uk/news/2012/09/03/archi-what.

Useful Resources

METHODS

Biggs, M. ed. (2002), *The Routledge Companion to Research in the Arts* (London: Routledge)

Clough, P. (2012), *A Student's Guide to Methodology* (London: Sage)

Groat, L. & D. Wang (2013), *Architectural Research Methods* 2nd ed. (New Jersey: Wiley)

Action research
Infed.org (2007), *Action Research* (infed. org: infed.org/mobi/action-research/)
McNiff, J. & Whitehead, J. (2002), *Action Research: Principles and Practice* (London: Routledge)

McNiff, J.& Whitehead, J. (2006), *All You Need to Know About Action Research* (London: Sage)

McNiff, J. (2002), *Action Research for Professional Development* 3rd ed. (Jean McNiff: www.jeanmcniff.com/ar-booklet. asp)

O'Brien, R. 'Um exame da abordagem metodológica da pesquisa ação [An Overview of the Methodological Approach of Action Research]' in Roberto Richardson, ed. *Teoria* (2001), *Teoria e Prática da Pesquisa Ação* [*Theory and Practice of Action Research*] (João Pessoa, Brazil: Universidade Federal da Paraíba); English version available at www.web. ca/~robrien/papers/arfinal.html

Pain, R. & Francis, P. (2003), 'Reflections on Participatory Research' *Area*, **35**

Whyte, W.F.E. (1991), *Participatory Action Research* (London: Sage)

Archaeology
C. Renfrew & P. Bahn (2012), *Archaeology: Theories, Methods and Practice* (London: Thames & Hudson), college. thamesandhudsonusa.com/college/ archaeology/archaeology6)

Building performance evaluation (BPE) and post-occupancy evaluation (POE)
BSRIA (n.d.) *Soft Landings* (BSRIA: www. bsria.co.uk/services/design/soft-landings)

Cabinet Office (2013), *Government Soft Landings* (Cabinet Office: www. bimtaskgroup.org/reports)

Malory-Hill, S., Preiser, W.F.E. & Watson, C.G. (2010), *Enhanced Building Performance* (New York: Routledge)

Usable Buildings Trust: www. usablebuildings.co.uk

Case study methodology
Yin, R. (2014) *Case Study Research: Design and Methods* 5th ed. (Thousand Oaks: Sage)

Coding software
AQUAD: www.aquad.de
CAT (Coding Analysis Toolkit), available from QDAP (Qualitative Data Analysis Program): cat.ucsur.pitt.edu
CATMA (Computer Aided Textual Markup & Analysis): www.catma.de

Risk assessment
See ethics procedures

Statistics
NIST/SEMATECH Engineering Statistics Handbook: www.itl.nist.gov/div898/handbook/

Statistics wikibook: en.wikibooks.org/wiki/Statistics

Whole life-cycle costing
Preiser, W. & J. Vischer (2005) *Assessing Building Performance* (Abingdon: Routledge)

Cooperative enquiry
Reason, P. & Heron, J. 'The Practice of Co-operative Inquiry: Research With Rather Than On People' in P. Reason & H. Bradbury, eds. (2010), *Handbook of Action Research: Participative Inquiry and Practice* (London: Sage: www.www.peterreason.eu/Papers/Handbook_Co-operative_Inquiry.pdf)

Reason, P. (2002), 'The Practice of Co-operative Inquiry' *Systematic Practice and Action Research*, **15**(3) www.peterreason.eu/Papers/CI_SprecialIssue/Editorial.pdf

Creative surveys
Butterworth, C. & S. Vardy (2008), 'Site-Seeing: Constructing the "Creative Survey"' *Field Journal*, **2**(1) www.field-journal.org/uploads/file/2008%20Volume%202%20/Site-Seeing_Butterworth,%20Vardy.pdf

Critical thinking
Critical Reasoning for Beginners (University of Oxford: podcasts.ox.ac.uk/series/critical-reasoning-beginners)

Critical Thinking – Advice and Resources on the Subject of Critical Thinking (University of Edinburgh: www.ed.ac.uk/schools-departments/institute-academic-development/postgraduate/taught/learning-resources/critical)

Design research
Design Research Techniques: designresearchtechniques.com

Fraser, M. (2013), *Design Research in Architecture: An Overview* (Farnham: Ashgate)

Environmental modelling
See *modelling*

Ethics procedures (including risk assessments)
Boddy, J., T. Neumann, S. Jennings, V. Morrow, P. Alderson, R. Rees & W. Gibson (n.d.) *The Research Ethics Guidebook: A Resource for Social Scientists* (Institute of Education, University of London: www.ethicsguidebook.ac.uk)

Economic and Social Research Council (2015), *Framework for Research Ethics* (ESRC: www.esrc.ac.uk/about-esrc/information/framework-for-research-ethics/)

University of Sheffield School of Architecture (n.d.) *Learning and Research Ethics* (University of Sheffield: www.sheffield.ac.uk/architecture/research/ethics)

Literature review (including systematic review and rapid appraisal)
GSR (2008), *Government Social Research Civil Services Rapid Evidence Assessment Toolkit* (GSR: www.civilservice.gov.uk/networks/gsr/resources-and-guidance)

Jesson, J.K., L. Matheson & F.M. Lacey (2011), *Doing Your Literature Review: Traditional and Systematic Techniques* (London: Sage)

Modelling
CarbonMixer: www.bobbygilbert.co.uk/CarbonMixer.html

Legion (pedestrian modelling): www.legion.com/legion-software

STEPS (pedestrian modelling): www.steps.mottmac.com

UK Climate Impact Programme (UKCIP): www.ukcip.org.uk

Participant observation
Kawulich, B.B. (2005), 'Participant Observation as a Data Collection Method' *Forum Qualitative Sozialforschung/Forum: Qualitative Social Research*, **6**(2) nbn-resolving.de/urn:nbn:de:0114-fqs0502430

Participatory action research
See *action research & design research*

Physical models and prototyping
See *design research*

Post-occupancy evaluation (POE)
See building performance evaluation.

Qualitative research
Strauss, A. & J. Corbin (1998) *Basics of Qualitative Research* 2nd ed. (London: Sage)

FUNDING

Research councils
Arts & Humanities Research Council: www.ahrc.ac.uk
Economic and Social Research Council: www.esrc.ac.uk
Engineering and Physical Sciences Research Council: www.epsrc.ac.uk

Other funders
British Academy: www.britac.ac.uk
European Cooperation in Science and Technology: www.cost.eu

Horizon 2020 (EU): ec.europa.eu/programmes/horizon2020/

Innovate UK: www.gov.uk/government/organisations/innovate-uk

Leverhulme Trust: www.leverhulme.ac.uk

NHBC Foundation: www.nhbcfoundation.org

RIBA Research Trust Awards: www.architecture.com/researchfunding

ARCHITECTURAL RESEARCH PRACTICE

Collins, E. (2014), *Architects and Research-based Knowledge: A Literature Review* (RIBA: www.architecture.com/research)

Coucill, L. et al. (2013), *RIBA Research Practice Guide* (RIBA: www.architecture.com/research)

Dye, A., A. Tait, F. Samuel eds (2014), *Review of University Research 2013* (RIBA & SCHOSA: www.architecture.com/research)

Samuel, F., et al Tait (2013), *RIBA Home Improvements: Housing Research in Practice* (RIBA: www.architecture.com/research)

Till, J. (2008), *What is Architectural Research? Architectural Research: Three Myths and One Model* (RIBA: www.architecture.com/research)

OTHER USEFUL RESOURCES

Architects' Council of England (2014), *The Architectural Profession in Europe* (Brussels: ACE, www.ace-cae.eu/fileadmin/New_Upload/7._Publications/Sector_Study/2014/EN/2014_EN_FULL.pdf)

The Alliance for Sustainable Building Products (ASBP) resource library: www.asbp.org.uk/resources

Passivhaus Trust: www.passivhaustrust.org.uk

RIBA (2015) *Design Quality and Performance* (RIBA: www.architecture.com/dqandp)

UK GBC (n.d.) *Pinpoint: Your Platform for Sustainability Resources* (UKGBC: pinpoint.ukgbc.org)

Credits

Index